THE PRINCETON REVIEW

COLLEGE
ADMISSIONS

CRACKING THE SYSTEM

THE PRINCETON REVIEW

COLLEGE

ADMISSIONS

CRACKING THE SYSTEM

Edited by Adam Robinson and John Katzman

 VILLARD BOOKS, NEW YORK 1991

Portions of Chapter Two were previously published in *The Princeton Review: Cracking the System: The SAT*.

Library of Congress Cataloging-in-Publication Data

Robinson, Adam.
    The Princeton review.

    1. Scholastic aptitude test—Study guides.
I. Katzman, John.
II. Title.
LB2353.57.R63   1987   328'.1664   85-51739
ISBN 0-394-75189-2

Manufactured in the United States of America
9   8   7   6   5

BOOK DESIGN BY BARBARA MARKS

FOREWORD
WHO ARE YOU GUYS?

In the fall of 1981, John founded The Princeton Review to prepare high school students for the Scholastic Aptitude Test. A year later, he began working with Adam, then a highly regarded private tutor. Our records indicate that our students improve their scores an average of 150 points. On the strength of these results, we have become the largest SAT course in the country. (We also prepare students for many other tests and offer private tutoring.)

WHAT MAKES YOU THINK YOUR COURSE IS SO GOOD?

Our classes are arranged according to ability. Classes are small (eight to twelve in a group), so each student receives personal attention. When a student doesn't understand something in class, we work with him in even smaller groups, and then one on one in tutoring. Our teachers are sharp and enthusiastic. They did well on their SATs and recently graduated from top colleges. You'll like them.

Unlike many coaches, we do not insist that you learn dozens of math theorems or memorize thousands of words. The more you know, of course, the better your score should be. But you cannot learn all of math and English in eight weeks. There is no way you can expect to know every word and equation that might show up on the SAT. Our approach is unique in that we will teach you how to attack a math or verbal question when you don't know how to solve it.

Finally, we do our homework. Every year we spend hundreds of thousands of dollars writing, improving and updating our course materials. The best research other courses have done is read our SAT book.

So our results are great. Some courses talk about their success stories, but are too embarrassed to mention their other students. We consistently achieve an average score improvement far greater than that of our largest competitor.

SO WHY ANOTHER BOOK ON COLLEGE ADMISSIONS?

Each year The Princeton Review sees tens of thousands of kids all over the country. Almost all of our students, after the SATs and the College Board Achievements are over, talk to us about other aspects of the college admissions process. They want to know how important interviews are. They want to know how to write application essays.

Dealing with so many students, we know their questions. We know their fears and confusions. We know the problems they face at school, and at home. And we feel that many of the books on college admissions sound as if they were written by people who have never been teenagers. These books seem directed more to parents than to students. We also feel that none of the books really tells it like it is. So we decided to write this book.

WHO SHOULD READ THIS BOOK?

Everybody! We're even sending a signed copy to Mick Jagger. Seriously, though, this book is written for high school students, primarily juniors and seniors (although even some sophomores have to take the PSAT these days). Finally, this book is written for any parents who want to understand what the whole college admissions process looks like to their teenage son or daughter.

Adam Robinson & John Katzman
August, 1987

ACKNOWLEDGMENTS

Adam and I have been SAT tutors for years, but the SAT is just one battle in the war. Our students have always asked us about other aspects of college admissions. Our education in college counseling came primarily through the patient work of Allen McLeod, Frank Leana, Carole Everett, and Mary Anne Schwalbe. We would also like to thank Beth Lohmann for her comments on learning-disabled students.

CONTENTS

INTRODUCTION

When college admissions officers, high school guidance counselors, and how-to-get-into-college books describe the perfect college applicant, they all describe more or less the same person. The ideal candidate, they say, has good grades, high scores, solid extracurricular activities (editor of the newspaper *and* captain of the football team), a fascinating after-school job (teaching English to immigrant children), terrific hobbies (managing a food relief program in Africa, playing medieval instruments), and a shelf filled with awards for everything from writing poetry to playing tennis. This candidate also lives on a farm, conducts unusual physics experiments, holds an elected political office in his town, restores old houses, coaches a Little League baseball team, and never once mentions SAT scores during an interview.

Real college applicants sometimes become depressed when they compare this super-applicant with their own meager selves. But their depression seldom lasts beyond the first day of their freshman year in college, when they notice that their roommates are just as ordinary as they are, and that virtually everyone else in their dormitory is too.

Although it is perfectly true that the ideal candidate described above would be accepted in a second by any college in the country, it is also true that ideal candidates are in short supply. You could probably squeeze all of them into a single freshman suite at Harvard. Even the most selective schools have to dip into the general run of humanity in order to fill their freshman classes. You shouldn't discount your chances simply because you feel you don't measure up to the admissions officers' ideal. There are a lot of boring adults in this country, and a lot of them went to college. (There are also a lot of people who, no matter how boring they seem to their friends, seem terribly interesting to admissions officers.)

At the same time—there's always a catch—the more closely you resemble the ideal candidate, the better your chances are going to be.

WHY YOU NEED THIS BOOK

This book contains advice about every aspect of the admissions process, from taking the SAT to selecting a photograph for your application. It tells you how to pick an appropriate college and how to go about finding financial aid. Most important, it gives you inside information that you'll never receive from anyone else.

If you're a high school junior or senior, you've probably already heard a lot of confusing advice about getting into college. Most of that confusing advice was probably offered with the very best of intentions. The fact is that people whose jobs and lives are devoted to college admissions tend to idealize what they do. When they tell you how the system works they are sometimes telling you only how they *wish* the system worked. Following their advice without question can sometimes hurt your chances.

THE PRINCETON REVIEW TO THE RESCUE

We at the Princeton Review have been helping high school students get into better colleges for six years. The most important help we give them is teaching them how to raise their SAT scores an average of 150 points. Many of our students raise their scores by more than 200 points. Our techniques for cracking the SAT are so successful that we are now the largest SAT-preparation school in the country. We have branches in about thirty cities (see the last page of this book for a list of our locations), and our coaching results have been written about in newspapers, discussed on *Nightline,* and described in *Time, Rolling Stone,* the *New York Times,* and other publications.

In addition to showing our students how to crack the SAT, we also give general information about applying to colleges. Much of this information comes from the many guidance counselors and admissions officers with whom we come into contact, but some of the best information comes from our old students. By studying all of this information together, we have developed a unique picture of how the college admissions process really works. This book is the distillation of what we have learned.

THE PRINCETON REVIEW APPROACH

Our techniques for doing better on the SAT work because they are based on the same principles that the SAT's publisher uses to create the test. We help our students by teaching them how to think like the people who write the questions.

Our techniques for getting into college work the same way. We can improve your admissions chances by teaching you how to think like the people who will be reading your application. When you understand how they think, you'll have a much easier time presenting yourself as the sort of person they want to admit.

Perhaps even more important, we will also teach you how most *applicants* think. The task you face when you fill out a college application is to make yourself stand out from hundreds and thousands of other high school seniors who are in many ways exactly like you. The more you sound like everybody else, the less chance you'll have of catching an admissions officer's attention.

THE JOE BLOGGS PRINCIPLE

"Standing out" may sound like an obvious strategy, but you'd be surprised at how few applicants actually manage to do it. In fact, some candidates never sound *more* like everybody else than when they're trying hardest to sound *different*. The reason for this is that most of us, unless we're extremely careful, tend to think in very predictable ways.

This simple fact is one of the keys to the success of the Princeton Review's method for cracking the SAT. In our SAT courses, we teach our students about an imaginary test-taker named Joe Bloggs. Joe Bloggs is the average American high school student. He has average grades and average SAT scores. There's a little bit of him in everyone, and there's a little bit of everyone in him. He isn't brilliant. He isn't dumb. He's exactly average.

On the SAT, Joe Bloggs thinks in a very, very predictable way. Because he does, we can teach our students how to score higher simply by teaching them to avoid the traps that Joe Bloggs invariably falls into. By the end of our course, our students can spot and avoid "Joe Bloggs answers"—that is, answer choices that are very appealing but incorrect—from a mile away.

JOE BLOGGS ALSO APPLIES TO COLLEGE

When Joe Bloggs applies to college, he is just as predictable as he is when he takes the SAT. Since there's at least a little bit of Joe Bloggs in all of us, we all tend to sound at least a little bit like him—and consequently like everybody else—when we fill out our applications.

SO, CUT IT OUT!

Much of the rest of this book is devoted to showing you, both directly and indirectly, how to conquer Joe Bloggs and make your application sound more like you and less like him. The fewer "Joe Bloggs answers" you make on your applications, the better your chances of being accepted at a selective school.

A SUBJECTIVE PROCESS

No matter how scientific and systematic your guidance counselor may sometimes sound, applying to college is a highly personal and subjective experience. Adults sometimes have trouble remembering exactly why they were initially attracted to the college they ended up happily attending. To be near the mountains? To be near a boyfriend? Because of something a parent said? Because of an advertisement in a magazine?

We can't give you a foolproof, step-by-step plan for getting into college. No one can. Even if you could be completely scientific about figuring out where you wanted to go and what you needed to do to get in, your case would still be in the hands of extremely subjective admissions officers. No matter how rational *you* are, your fate could still end up being decided by a grumpy person whose car broke down that morning.

Since the admissions process is so subjective, for both applicants and admissions officers, we aren't going to offer you a hard-and-fast formula for acceptance. Such formulas just don't work. Our advice is less scientific, but more useful. We'll give you the kind of information you need to avoid the pitfalls that await the uninformed student. We'll give you insight into the minds of the people who will decide whether to admit or reject you. We'll teach you how not to be Joe Bloggs.

DON'T GET CARRIED AWAY

Going to college is a big step for most people, but it isn't the most important thing in the world. There are a lot of happy, successful people who never went to college. There are also a lot of unhappy, unsuccessful people with college degrees. Who you are inside is more important than where, or whether, you went to college.

If we sometimes sound as though we've forgotten that, it's only because we believe that if you do want to go to college, you have a right to know how the system really works. If your favorite extracurricular activity is one that we say doesn't impress admissions officers, that doesn't mean you should find something else to do after school. But you do need to know how the admissions officers think. That's why we wrote this book.

HOW THIS BOOK IS ORGANIZED

There are two kinds of colleges: the ones you want to go to and the ones you can get into. With luck and a little planning, you'll find substantial overlap between the two categories.

The first chapter of this book is devoted to helping you think about where you want to go to college. This is a personal decision, of course, but we can make it easier for you by giving you information that students aren't usually given and by helping you avoid some common traps and pitfalls.

Most of the rest of the book is devoted to helping you maximize your chances of being accepted at the colleges that appeal to you. Separate sections or chapters are devoted to such important factors as test scores, interviews, application essays, and your high school record.

We suggest that you read the book straight through and then refer back to particular chapters as you need them.

IS IT TOO LATE? IS IT TOO EARLY?

Your parents may have begun thinking about where they wanted you to go to college on the day you were born, or even sooner. You may not be entirely convinced that you need to think about it yet. Or, you may think about it all the time. When is the right time to think about going to college?

Well, senior year is a bit late. Application deadlines arrive awfully quickly if you don't start writing to colleges before the first semester of twelfth grade. If you're already a senior and you haven't done anything yet, spend the rest of the afternoon reading this book and get cracking.

If you're a ninth- or tenth-grader, you're probably rushing things, although it's never too early to start earning straight A's in Advanced Placement courses. (If you're taking a course like biology or chemistry, you may also need to take an Achievement test now, while the material is still fresh.) This is too early, however, to write away for information from colleges.

The best time to start thinking seriously about college is your junior year. By that time, you'll have a fairly good idea of what your high-school grade point average and class rank are likely to be, and you'll probably be starting to have some test scores, too. With those pieces of information, you'll begin to develop an idea of the sort of schools to which you can realistically hope to be admitted.

WHO AM I, ANYWAY?

In writing this book, we have assumed that you are interested in attending a selective college. By "selective college" we mean a school that rejects significant numbers of applicants. This is common sense. If the college you want to attend accepts everyone who applies, you shouldn't need to read a book to tell you how to get in.

The advice in this book is generally geared towards the more selective of the selective schools—the fifty or sixty colleges in the country that are the hardest to get into. Much of the same advice applies, though, to colleges below the top fifty or sixty. It also applies, with certain variations that we'll tell you about later, to state colleges and universities. Just remember that there are colleges with many different degrees of selectivity, and an applicant who is rejected by one school may be welcomed with open arms (and possibly offered a scholarship) by another.

If we sometimes seem to fall into the "perfect applicant" fallacy that we mentioned at the beginning of this introduction —by describing super-candidates who couldn't possibly exist— keep in mind that selectivity is a broad spectrum. Your task is to make yourself the best candidate you can be, given what you have to offer.

IS THIS A GOOD TIME TO BE APPLYING TO COLLEGE?

You've probably heard something about the effect that the aging of the so-called Baby Boom generation has had on the college admissions process. The Baby Boom was a large increase in the birth rate that took place in the late nineteen-forties and early nineteen-fifties: When American soldiers came home from World War II, they got married and started families all at once. When the Baby Boom babies began to turn eighteen, in the nineteen-sixties, colleges began to be swamped with applications, and new colleges started up to take care of all those new students.

By now, most of the Baby Boom babies have long since graduated from college. That means that there are fewer teenagers applying to college every year than there used to be.

Does That Mean It's Easier to Get into College Than It Was Ten Years Ago?

The answer is yes and no. It is true that most colleges are probably easier to get into than they used to be. But it is also true that the most elite and prestigious colleges are harder to get into than they used to be.

Why is that?

As the cost of a private college education has begun to climb out of sight, parents have become increasingly reluctant to shell out $60,000 or $70,000 or more to send a child to a distinguished but sub-Ivy League liberal arts college. They might happily spend that much money to send you to Harvard, Stanford, or MIT—but not to Grinnell or Occidental. I'll pay for Yale, some parents are saying, but if you don't get in, you're going to the state university.

Good News, Bad News

What does all this mean? Several things. First, the Harvards, Stanfords, and MITs of the world are becoming harder to get into, because they're attracting so many applications. Second, the Grinnells and Occidentals of the world are becoming somewhat easier to get into—at least for students who can pay their own way. Third, many state universities are becoming harder to get into, even for in-state applicants. Fourth, many colleges, even some of the most prestigious ones, are spending enormous sums to market themselves to prospective students, sometimes without much regard for truth in advertising.

All of these factors make good college planning more important than ever. Start reading.

COLLEGE
ADMISSIONS

CRACKING THE SYSTEM

CHAPTER 1

PICKING COLLEGES

"*My first two weeks at Middlebury, I was miserable. I had wanted to go to Williams but I didn't get in. I moped around. Everybody seemed dumb. All the girls seemed ugly. But then, gradually, I started to like the place. By the time I graduated, I couldn't believe that anybody would want to go to a school as stuffy as Williams. Now I help raise money for Middlebury.*"

Before you can be admitted to the college of your choice, you have to decide what the college of your choice is. Your decision will be influenced heavily by some factors over which you have no control—such as your parents' income and the grades you've already earned. It will also be influenced, perhaps decisively, by factors that are entirely personal. Most high school students change their minds many times. Some don't decide until the day their deposits are due.

IS THERE A SCIENTIFIC SYSTEM?

Many high school guidance counselors and how-to-get-into-college books recommend that students construct incredibly elaborate charts and tables ranking different schools according to such factors as size, location, curriculum, atmosphere, and so on. School A wins so many points for having a home economics department, School B loses points for not allowing freshmen to park on campus.

If you're the sort of person who makes a lot of lists and enjoys ranking things on scales of one to ten, you'll undoubtedly make a chart comparing possible colleges. If you aren't such a person, you probably won't, and there's nothing that anyone could tell you that would make you more likely to do it. Our experience has been that students almost never make fancy charts like the ones in the guidance books. One of our students told us that she spent most of an afternoon making an elaborate filing system for college materials. She bought a cardboard Transfile and filled it with folders and dividers. Then it sat. After a week, she was stuffing dirty clothes into it.

Furthermore, students who do make complicated charts seldom learn anything very meaningful from them. Unless you are intimately familiar with the schools you're considering, your evaluations of "atmosphere," "academic rigor," "class size," and so on won't mean very much. Does Oberlin deserve a five or an eight for "faculty advising programs"? Even Oberlin would have trouble answering that one. And even if you could answer it, what would your answer tell you? Just what sort of "faculty advising" do you think you're going to need?

SO, WHAT DO I DO INSTEAD?

No one can make your college decision for you, and no one can tell you exactly how to go about making it. The purpose of this chapter is not to give you a step-by-step program for arriving at a mythical "perfect" college, but rather to give you some important information that should help you clarify your thoughts. This is information that Princeton Review students have found useful over the years. It is *not* information that guidance counselors, parents, teachers, or admissions officers usually give.

HOW TO BEGIN

Most high school students have at least a few schools in mind as they begin to think about college. Your father wants you to go to Vanderbilt, your mother went to the University of Florida, your brother is at Occidental, someone once told you something nice about Bard, your guidance counselor thinks you ought to go to a junior college. You can start your selection process by thinking about these schools. If you don't want to go to Vanderbilt, you're going to have to come up with an explanation that will sound reasonable to your father. ("Dad, I'm just too dumb.") In thinking about why you don't want to go to Vanderbilt, you will make a lot of discoveries about where you do want to go.

Don't worry if your search for the perfect college seems unsystematic, even haphazard. In the end, every decision about which college to attend is subjective.

TWO QUESTIONS, TWO POINTS

We have found that it is helpful to ask yourself two general questions about every school you want to consider:
1. Do I want to go to school here for four years?
2. Do I want to live here for four years?
Surprisingly, the second question often ends up being more important than the first. There are lots of colleges where you

can get a good education; there are only a few where you can live in a chalet and ski after class.

Most people are pretty good at developing a general picture of what particular colleges are like. Where they get into trouble is in the details that don't seem significant until after they enroll. Here we're going to give you some specific things to think about. These are by no means the only criteria that you should take into consideration in evaluating colleges. But they are ones that you are least likely to think of by yourself.

Seventeen Factors (in No Particular Order) That Do and Don't Matter

1. MONEY

A lot of colleges cost a lot of money. If your parents aren't rich, the cost will make a big difference. Even when colleges say they don't pay attention to applicants' financial need in accepting and rejecting students, they really do. (See Chapter Seven.)

How much money your parents can afford to spend on college is going to affect not only where you go to school but also what your life is like once you get there. Do you mind juggling several outside jobs with your schoolwork? Do you mind graduating with a heavy debt? Do you mind going to a school where virtually all of the students have more money than you do? There's a lot of financial aid out there, but few scholarships pay the entire bill, and most have strings attached. One of the first things you have to do is sit down with your parents and talk fully and honestly about the bottom line.

2. DISTANCE

When you're calculating college costs, don't forget to add in the cost of transportation. Trotting back and forth between school and home can run up a big bill, particularly if school and home aren't located on heavily traveled discount air routes. Don't decide that you'll save money by staying at school during all your vacations. Students stranded on empty campuses during big holidays are among the most depressed people in the world. Some colleges even assign staff members to look after such students in order to make certain they don't throw themselves out of windows on Christmas Eve. Spending Christmas away from home may sound like a great idea to you now, but a rough first semester as a freshman could change your mind.

3. LOCATION

City or country? Can you stand four years of funny accents? Do you mind living on the fringes of a high-crime area? Do you mind not seeing first-run movies? Do you mind living in a town that has no good restaurants?

These questions have nothing to do with *education*, but they are not frivolous. Many college applicants forget that they are selecting not only a school but also a place to live. Be sure you want to live there before you sign up to go. Also remember that if you're going to have to work your way through school, a big city will offer more employment opportunities than a small town. It will also make it easier to find jobs that won't bring you into constant contact with your schoolmates, if that would bother you.

4. CLIMATE

If you grew up in Florida, you're probably going to have trouble adjusting to winters in Maine. You're also going to have to buy a lot of new clothes. Weather can make a big difference in your state of mind. If rainy days make you feel gloomy, you may want to think twice about going to college in Oregon.

5. LIVING ARRANGEMENTS

At least as important as where you live is how you live. Colleges differ greatly in the housing they offer. Some offer none at all. Some don't permit off-campus living. Do you mind showering in front of a dozen other people? Are single rooms available for freshmen? If it matters to you, find out.

It may sound silly, but things like the location of freshman dormitories can make a bigger impression on a freshman's mind than the quality of freshman courses. Your living arrangements will influence who your friends are, how you spend your free time, how early you have to get up in the morning, and how late you can stay out at night.

Here's how one of our former students puts it: "The best thing about college for me isn't college, it's my apartment. After freshman year, you're allowed to live off campus. My parents give me what they would have spent on room and board, and I use it to pay my rent and buy my food. I sleep in a bed I bought for ten dollars, I make my own breakfast and my own coffee, and when school's over for the day I drink a beer in my own living room. I feel like an adult. And my grades are better too."

That's just the way one student thinks about it. You might be a lot happier living in a dormitory with a lot of other students. But this particular student's college experience would have been a lot different if he had attended a school that didn't let sophomores live off campus. You can't anticipate exactly how you'll feel about this sort of thing, but by now you know enough about your likes and dislikes to have a reasonably good idea of how you might like to live.

Life in virtually all freshman dormitories is alike in some respects: It's loud, messy, crowded, uncomfortable, and often a lot of fun. There are important differences, though, and understanding them before you make a commitment can lead to a happier few years.

6. WHERE YOUR FRIENDS GO

Going to college with high school friends can be great or terrible, depending. On the one hand, going away to a college where you know nobody is one of the few opportunities you'll have in life to wipe the slate clean on the person you used to be. Even better, it comes at a time when many people are very eager to wipe the slate clean. If you don't know anyone on campus, no one will know about the time the captain of the football team hung you from a coat hook by the band of your underpants. On the other hand, having a close friend nearby can make the first weeks of freshman year less frightening. Freshmen with ready-made friends sometimes look like upperclassmen to other freshmen.

You'll make more new friends if you don't have the old gang

to fall back on. Feelings of freshman alienation usually don't last beyond the first couple of weeks. People also change at college. The kind of people you like to hang around with won't necessarily stay the same.

7. WHERE YOUR BOYFRIEND OR GIRLFRIEND GOES

A fair number of people marry their high school sweethearts, but many, many more of them don't. Before you decide to attend a certain college in order to be with your current boyfriend or girlfriend, think through the consequences.

Freshman year in college can put a huge strain on a high school romance. Dormitory life is fun and liberating. Even small colleges offer temptations that high schools don't. It takes a strong relationship to survive the dramatic change in lifestyle that freshman year in college means to most people. We knew two students who had been going steady since eighth grade. They ordered catalogs together, picked colleges together, filled out their applications together, and enrolled in the same school. Then, a week into freshman year, they broke up. They spent most of the first semester just trying to avoid each other on campus, which was hard, because they were at a small school. The boy ended up transferring.

Having a steady boyfriend or girlfriend nearby can limit your ability to make new friends of both sexes. If you spend all your time with your high school sweetheart, you're not going to meet a lot of other people. Many people's fondest memories of freshman year involve informal group activities in which no clear couples were differentiated.

Adults tend to say that if a relationship is meant to last, it will last. This isn't necessarily true, but a strong relationship will survive some distance. Our advice is to attend college a few hours away from each other.

8. TRENDINESS

Every year there are a few hot schools to which everyone seems to apply. Hot schools are usually good colleges that are suddenly perceived as being easier to get into than the very best colleges. As a result, they attract a huge number of applications and sometimes actually become *harder* to get into than the best colleges. In recent years Brown and Williams, to name two, have been very, very hot.

Remember what we said about Joe Bloggs. When Joe Bloggs hears about a hot school, his reaction is, "Hey I'd better apply, too!" But the more people who want to go to a school, the more people who are going to be rejected. The movie with the longest line may be a great movie, but it won't matter if you can't get a seat.

This doesn't mean you shouldn't apply to a hot school. It just means you shouldn't depend on getting in, even if your credentials would ordinarily make you a strong contender. Pay attention to the colleges your classmates are applying to and use your judgment. If you decide to apply to a certain school because you read an interesting article about it in *Time*, remember that several million other people will have read about it too.

9. STUDENT/FACULTY RATIO AND AVERAGE CLASS SIZE

If it's possible to deduce anything important from a student/faculty ratio, we don't know what it is. Don't worry about it. Many colleges fudge their statistics anyway.

Much the same can be said for average class size, another statistic to which applicants pay too much attention. Course quality is much more important than class size (although it's also much harder to assess, unfortunately). Huge courses taught by great teachers are more rewarding than tiny courses taught by morons. In small classes you often have to spend an inordinate amount of time listening to the opinions of your classmates. Some professors who shine in big lecture courses are unbearable in small seminars.

One of our students summed it up for us nicely: "I came from a big high school where there were never enough desks, and one of the things I cared about most when I applied to college was class size—I wanted them small. But the funny thing was, my very worst class freshman year was an English class that only had six students in it and that usually met in the professor's living room. The professor was a creep, and the students were creeps, and there was nowhere to hide. And my favorite course was a freshman science course that met in an auditorium and had about 500 students in it. The professor was like a great actor, and every lecture was exciting."

Also remember that student/faculty ratio and average class size mean even less if the courses you plan to take don't fit the usual pattern. If you are planning to major in Greek and the university to which you're applying only has seven Greek majors, your classes are going to be small no matter what the statistics say.

10. COURSE CATALOGS

Some students try to compare colleges on the basis of catalogs of course offerings. As college freshmen soon discover, though, course catalogs are works of fiction. Courses that sound great on the printed page are often hideous in reality. The course that makes you want to go to Antioch may be canceled by the time you get there. Who the teacher is usually makes more difference than what is being taught, and it's almost impossible to evaluate the teachers until you're actually on campus and taking their courses.

Of course, if you have special academic interests, you need to be certain that the colleges you are considering can satisfy them. If you want to major in Russian, be sure the schools you apply to have Russian departments. (Remember, many students don't stay with the majors they start out with.)

11. FACULTY CREDENTIALS

You may very well have been told that a good way to compare colleges is to look in the back of course catalogs to see how many professors have Ph.D.s. Don't bother. The catalogs don't provide nearly enough information about faculty members for you to make meaningful comparisons. The general prestige of a college will give you some idea of the quality of the faculty, but lists of where professors went to school and what degrees they earned won't help you. Nor will average age, percentage of tenured professors, or any other sweeping statistic that doesn't take account of individuals.

12. VIEWBOOKS

Many colleges supplement their catalogs with viewbooks, brochures, and other publications. You can get some idea of what
a campus is like by looking at the pictures, but there is no
college in existence that really looks as good as its viewbook. A
viewbook is an advertisement. The college hopes that it will put
you in the mood to buy. Four magnificent years in downtown
Los Angeles for just sixty thousand dollars! You should be just
as skeptical of a viewbook as you are of the claims in a television
commercial. You will never find a college that has the same
proportion of happy students, magnificent scenery, and beautiful weather that it depicts in its brochures.

Colleges also use their viewbooks to spell out their educational philosophies. Most colleges have interchangeable philosophies—"a firm commitment to the liberal arts," and so on
—but some colleges do have unusual programs or other specialized approaches to education. These will always be explained in the viewbook or other brochure. If you don't want to
spend a year building a yurt, don't apply to a college that requires it.

13. WHAT YOUR PARENTS THINK

Unless you're still earning residuals from those peanut butter
commercials you did as a child, you're probably going to need
your parents' help in financing your education. Don't alienate
them by telling them right off the bat that you don't care what
they think. Subtle persuasion is more effective. If you want to
go to an Ivy League university and they want to economize by
sending you to the local community college, appeal to their
vanity. Try persuading them at least to let you apply. If you get
in, your case will be strengthened; if you don't, there's nothing
to fight about.

A mistake many high school students make is letting their
parents' wishes *prevent* them from applying to schools they
would actually enjoy attending. Don't *not* apply to a particular
college just because your mother wants you to go there. Think
these things out rationally, and plot strategies. Also do your

homework. If money is the problem, find out about sources of financial aid *before* you talk to your parents. (See Chapter Seven.)

Remember that many students change their minds often about where they want to go to college. If you are determined to do battle with your parents, make sure you're fighting over a school that genuinely means something to you. If you fight with your parents and win, you may find it difficult to back down later. Are you that set on going to school three thousand miles from home?

14. WHAT YOUR COLLEGE COUNSELOR THINKS

Most counselors are knowledgeable and really do care. Listen to what they have to say. While there are a lot of good college counselors out there, however, there are also some overworked if not bad ones. A counselor may have *hundreds* of students to advise on personal, career, and academic concerns, not to mention college planning. Moreover, even the best counselor cannot be expected to know about all of the programs and departments at the colleges around the country.

If you are applying to a college or program outside your counselor's experience, you'll have to do some research on your own. If you feel you cannot talk to your counselor because he or she is overworked, you should consider seeking the help of a good independent college adviser.

Here are a few things to watch out for:

▪ Does your counselor know you by sight? Is he or she familiar with the courses and extracurricular activities you're taking? Remember: Counselors cannot read minds. It's your job to let your counselor know all of your activities, achievements, and goals. Admissions officers are unimpressed by letters of recommendation written by counselors who obviously don't know the students they're recommending.

▪ Does your high school regularly send graduates to colleges equal in caliber to the ones you want to attend? If not, your counselor may not be much help in advising you.

▪ How many students is your counselor handling? If he or she has 272 students, don't expect that much personal attention.

According to Alan McLeod, one of the top counselors in New York, counselors should be working with no more than fifty students at a time.

▪ Are the publications in your counselor's office extensive and up to date? Only the most recent brochures provide reliable information.

▪ Is your counselor knowledgeable about SAT and ACT testing dates, registration procedures, and so on? Most counselors are, but if yours is not, you're going to have to be responsible about getting this information yourself. You can contact ETS at (609) 771-7435 or (415) 654-1200, and the ACT at (319) 337-1000.

▪ Does your counselor tend to recommend the same few colleges again and again to you and your classmates? Did he tell the smartest kid in your class to apply to colleges you've never heard of? Some counselors act as though there were only three or four colleges in the country. Beware. Dr. John S. Yaegel, former president of the New Jersey School Counselor Association, says to be sure you ask your counselor to investigate a wide scope of challenging colleges with you, including some "safeties" where you know you'll be admitted.

15. SAT AVERAGES

One of the first things students do when they begin to think about college is to look up colleges in one of the big directories (such as the College Board's *College Handbook* or the Barron's two-volume *Profiles of American Colleges*) and eliminate schools whose average SAT or ACT score is higher than their own test scores. This can be dangerous, for a number of complicated and sometimes contradictory reasons:

▪ An average is an average, not a cutoff. If a college's average verbal SAT is 550, that means that half of the students scored *below* 550.

▪ Colleges lie about their SAT averages. The colleges themselves supply the numbers printed in the directories, and sometimes they exaggerate. All colleges want to look selective. Sometimes they do that by inflating their averages. They may do it by giving the average scores of the students they admit rather than of those who enroll. They may also do it by using only their students' best scores. (A school can inflate its average by admitting a lot of high-scoring students it knows will probably end up going somewhere else.) They may do it by eliminating the scores of minorities, who as a group do worse on admissions tests than whites do, from the totals. They may do it simply by reporting higher scores than they receive.

Schools' fibbing about SAT averages can work both for you and against you. On the one hand, a school may be easier to get into than its claimed average may seem to suggest. On the other hand, a school may be so worried about its SAT average that it avoids students with lower-than-average scores.

▪ Some colleges are actually *harder* to get into than their published SAT averages suggest. If an average includes the scores of minority students (which, as we said, tend to be lower), the effective cutoff for nonminority students will be higher than it seems to be. We'll tell you more about this in Chapter Six.

▪ If you've only taken the PSAT, comparing your scores with SAT averages will probably be misleading. Most students' scores go up when they take the SAT. See Chapter Two. Our advice is to look at the SAT averages in the guides, but to use a wide net. Any school whose average is within 250 points of your own composite should pass this test.

16. SCHOOL SIZE

The size of the college you attend can have a big effect on your experience there. Big schools have more activities, more facilities, more students, more everything. It's easier to stand out at a small school, but harder to melt into the crowd. At a big school you have to take a greater responsibility for planning your own education and securing your own living arrangements than you do at a small school.

You shouldn't have any trouble thinking of plenty of differences between big and small schools. Think of the differences between living in a town and living in a city.

But some differences between large and small schools are exaggerated. For example, many high school students say that they don't want to go to a small school because they won't be able to "meet enough people." Now, let's be serious. How many people do you know now? How many do you think you'll meet at a university with 50,000 students? In fact, students often meet more people at smaller schools than they do at big ones, simply because the overall environment isn't as intimidating. Furthermore, big schools are usually broken down into smaller units. Even though you attend a huge university, you may spend virtually all of your time with the fewer than 4,000 students in the undergraduate college of arts and sciences.

Size is important, but it's sometimes not as important as most high school students tend to think it is. Stop thinking like most high school students!

17. LIBRARY SIZE

The number of volumes in a college's library can make a difference, but think about this carefully. It is not unknown for a high school student to cross a college off his list because its library is "too small," then go to a college with a bigger library and not set foot inside it during four years except to use the bathroom.

How Do I Find Out About Colleges?

There are a lot of sources of information about particular colleges. (In fact, there are too many.) Here are some of the most important ones and what we think of them:

1. VISITS

There are two kinds of college trip, and both may have places in your planning.

The first kind is a trip with your parents, usually taken during the summer between your junior and senior years. Frankly, you're not going to learn a lot (for one thing, most of the schools you visit won't be in session), but it's a good chance to get to know your folks better and share your thoughts about college.

The second kind of trip is usually more helpful. This is a trip you take with a friend during the fall of your senior year. You may even have an older friend or a sibling already enrolled at a college you think you might want to attend. (If you don't know anyone on campus, the admissions office will often arrange for you to stay with students.) Hang around in the student union, visit some classes, buy a sweatshirt at the bookstore, and try to get the feel of the place.

Many guidance counselors and how-to-get-into-college books recommend that you strike up conversations with passing students and ask them what they think of their school. If you feel comfortable talking to strangers, go ahead. But if you don't, don't worry about it. Simply keeping your ears open will probably be as helpful. And don't worry that everyone will know you're a high school student. They won't.

Visits to nearby colleges are often less intimidating and easier to arrange than treks to distant parts of the country. Be sure to leave your parents at home. Most admissions offices arrange campus tours, often conducted by students. If you're interested in joining one of these, call ahead.

When you visit colleges, be careful that you don't let yourself be swayed by factors that don't really matter. Don't decide to go to a school just because someone smiled at you on the steps of the library. And don't decide not to go there just because it was cold and rainy on the day of your visit.

(Many colleges offer, and some colleges strongly suggest that you have, on-campus interviews. If so, a trip may be even more helpful or necessary. We'll tell you more about these interviews in Chapter Four.)

2. GUIDES AND DIRECTORIES

Reading the big directories like *Barron's* and *The College Handbook* is a little like reading the phone book. Two of the smaller, more subjective guides (the *Yale Daily News's Insider's Guide to Colleges* and Edward H. Fiske's *Selective Guide to Colleges*) can be fascinating. The essays in Fiske's book are particularly accurate. All these books can help you form an idea, however, and the big directories can answer specific questions about academic programs and requirements.

The big directories have another valuable use. They are an

authoritative source for mailing addresses. Always consult them when you write away for information and applications. Big universities often have separate admissions departments for undergraduates, graduate, and other schools. If you write to the University of Michigan and simply say, "Send me an application," they won't know what you mean.

Don't go out and buy copies of all of these books. You may not even need to buy any; most libraries carry them. When you need more specific information, go to the library or to your guidance counselor's office.

3. THE COLLEGES THEMSELVES, IN PERSON

Many admissions officers spend a lot of time traveling around the country and talking with high school students. If a college is popular with students at your high school, an admissions officer may schedule a meeting right at your school. Other admissions officers conduct regional information sessions or take part in college fairs.

These meetings are sometimes more useful to colleges than they are to high school students. Colleges use them to promote themselves and attract applications. You can pick up information at these meetings, but you should always keep in mind that the colleges are trying to sell you something.

You should also keep in mind that the impression you make at these meetings can have a bearing on your chances for admission. You will probably be asked to sign your name in a book or fill out an information card when you arrive. If you make a bad impression (because you didn't wear shoes and asked a stupid question), the admissions officer conducting the meeting may remember you. Admissions officers often take notes on the meetings they conduct, sometimes making notations directly on the information cards filled out by the students. (They do this even when they say they don't.)

It would be a mistake to try to stand out at one of these meetings: Don't try to monopolize the admissions officer's attention and certainly don't brag about your SAT scores. The most important thing is not to make an indelibly bad impression. You don't want to start the admissions process with a strike against you.

4. THE COLLEGES THEMSELVES, BY MAIL

Earlier in this chapter, we told you not to pay too much attention to the rosy pictures colleges present of themselves in their viewbooks and other brochures. Even so, there is some important information that you can glean from these publications. They will tell you about living arrangements, academic and other requirements (both for admission and for graduation), special programs, costs, financial aid opportunities and procedures, and other factors that will influence your decision.

You can receive all this information simply by writing to the colleges to which you are interested in applying. You should do this no later than the summer after your junior year (and no earlier than the last semester of your junior year). You don't need to write a letter. Just send a postcard to the admissions office requesting information about the school and an application. Keep it brief, but don't forget your name and address. Send these cards to every school in which you have any interest at all—at least ten.

No college is going to admit or reject you on the basis of your request for an application, but your postcard could end up in your application folder. For that reason, you should type or write neatly (good typing is always preferable to good handwriting in every part of your application). Don't make a big sloppy crossout or a spelling error that will catch the eye of every admissions officer who flips through your file.

Colleges respond to requests for information and applications in many different ways. Some will send you an application immediately. Others will send you a letter explaining that a catalog and other materials are being mailed to you separately. Others will send a preliminary application or a card requesting a few additional pieces of information, such as your full name and the name of your high school. Most will write to you more than once. When you're on a school's mailing list, you can expect to stay on it for quite a while. Keep track of all this stuff, and keep the applications themselves in a separate file that won't get beaten up and banged around.

WHAT, ME WORRY?

It's important to remember that most students end up liking where they go to college. The student who is crushed to have been rejected by Princeton ends up loving Oberlin and even being happy that the fates kept her from being accepted by what had once been her first choice. In many ways, the most important thing about college is the one characteristic that virtually all colleges have in common: They are communities of young people living on their own without many serious responsibilities. You'll never get another chance to do it, and you'll probably enjoy it almost anywhere you have a chance.

On the other hand, where you go to college can be very important. In addition to determining where you spend the next four years of your life, where you go to school can determine where you work after graduation, whom you marry, where you live, and who your lifelong friends are. A degree from Wharton really can make it easier to get a good job after graduation; spending four years in a glamorous state like Colorado or Hawaii really can be a lot of fun. You should make your college decision carefully and with a clear head. Don't make your decision simply in order to please (or infuriate) someone else.

If you begin to think that you won't be able to go on living unless you get into (let's say) Yale, get a hold of Yale's faculty directory and see where its professors went to college. Some of them went to Yale, some to Harvard, some to other Ivy League schools, but many of them went to exactly the sort of colleges that you think are beneath you. If those colleges are good enough for Yale, might they not also be good enough for you? You should approach college selection thoughtfully, but not with a conviction that your life hangs in the balance.

QUESTIONS AND ANSWERS

My parents want to hire an independent counselor to advise me. Is this a good idea?

Independent guidance counselors are becoming quite popular, particularly in areas (such as New York City) where there are high concentrations of competitive high schools and anxious parents. The fees charged by these counselors can be very high—sometimes more than two thousand dollars. Some parents believe, though, that no expense is too great if it will give their children an edge.

There are a lot of bad independent counselors out there (everybody's an expert, as you've probably already discovered). We heard of one man who claimed to have a friend on the admissions committee at Brown and offered a money-back guarantee of acceptance in return for a thousand dollars. This person did nothing but collect checks. Some of his "advisees" got in; most didn't. He returned the money of those who were rejected and pocketed the rest.

Some of the best independent counselors we know are former admissions officers from top selective colleges or former guidance counselors from first-rate high schools. These people can be very, very helpful. They can show you how to present your case in the best possible light, and they can give you good advice about which schools you should be considering.

Don't expect an independent counselor to pull strings for you. In fact, you shouldn't let an independent counselor write a recommendation for you or contact a school in your behalf. Most selective colleges don't like independent counselors, and students who have them can seem pushy. If you hire an independent, keep it to yourself. Listen to what he or she has to say, but don't let colleges know you have a paid helper.

Stay away from any independent counselor who promises to write your essay for you. That's cheating. You should expect a counselor to help you polish your essay, though, and to help you with grammar, spelling, and the appropriateness of your topic.

How many colleges should I apply to?

Six.

Actually, we just made that up. But six is probably a pretty good number. If you apply to more than that, you'll have to devote your life to it. Besides, nobody needs more than six choices.

Be certain that one of the schools you apply to is a school you are absolutely positive you'll be admitted to—a safety school. (Also be certain that your safety school is a school you wouldn't mind attending if you had to. Stranger things have happened.)

Even if you are absolutely positive that there are only two colleges in the world that you could conceivably bear to attend, apply to a few more as well. You could change your mind later on.

Who makes admissions decisions?

Different colleges have different systems. At some, undergraduates and faculty members play a role. At others, all decisions are made by a small handful of professionals. At still others, decisions are made democratically by large committees.

Here's the way the admissions process works at one top Ivy League school: Students' applications are given a preliminary reading and assigned two ratings, personal and academic. Each is scored on a scale of 1 to 4, with 1 being the best. The academic rating is based on, in equal parts, grades and standardized test scores. The personal rating is based on extracurricular activities, interviews, and recommendations. If the combined rating is 4 or less, the student is assigned a "likely"; 6 or more is an "unlikely"; 5 is a "possible."

Even if you know the exact composition of the admissions office at a school to which you are applying, that knowledge won't do you much good. More important than who they are is what they are: tired of reading boring applications.

How hard is it to transfer?

Generally speaking, the more prestigious a school is, the harder it is to transfer into. The reason for this isn't difficult to understand: There just aren't a lot of students who leave schools like Harvard and Yale, and if they don't leave there isn't room for transfers. The easiest schools to transfer into are the ones with high attrition rates—but then you have to ask yourself, why are all those other students leaving?

Transferring isn't impossible, though. In fact, many colleges have found that transfer students do unusually well. A few rules apply:

• Schools almost never accept transfer students who have completed more than two years in another college.

• Your college transcript will be the most important part of your application folder. SAT scores are used to predict college grades; once you *have* college grades, the scores are less important.

• Colleges typically do require test scores for transfer students, though. Most transfer applicants simply submit the scores they received in high school. We recommend, however, that you take the test again. You'll almost certainly score higher than you did in high school.

• Colleges don't make transfer decisions until after they've filled the freshman class. This means you probably won't hear whether you've been admitted until the summer, even the late summer. Be sure you have a contingency plan ready if you get turned down.

• Colleges usually expect transfer applicants to have clear, compelling academic reasons for wanting to switch schools. Simply being unhappy at your present school isn't enough. The best reason is a strong desire to pursue a course of study that isn't offered at your present school. You'll have to make your case in detail, and you'll have to be convincing. A transfer applicant, unlike a freshman applicant, can't get away with being "undecided" about academic goals.

• Your application has to make sense. It is virtually impossible to transfer to Harvard from Princeton or Yale, for example. Harvard's admissions office will decide, justifiably, that you are attending a very good school right now and that you don't need to be rescued.

What is a waiting list?

All selective colleges admit more students than they have room for. They do this because they know that many of the students they admit won't actually enroll. Guessing how many students will enroll is a very inexact science. To protect themselves, most colleges have waiting lists. An applicant who is "wait-listed" is one who may be admitted if enough other students decide to go somewhere else.

If you're wait-listed at a school you want to attend, you can usually help your case substantially. Write a letter reaffirming your desire to attend the school. Ask you guidance counselor to call the admissions office. Send a letter describing any honors you've won since you sent in your application. If you have a connection, pull it. When colleges admit students from waiting lists, they almost always give preference to students who have made it clear they really want to attend.

At the very most popular and selective schools, admissions from waiting lists are sometimes few and far between. Your guidance counselor can get a feel for your chances by making a phone call. Don't knock yourself out if the situation is hopeless, but remember that the places that do open up usually go to the students who make themselves heard.

You (OK, maybe one of your parents) bought this book because you're going to college next year. Everyone you know expects you to go to college next year. Your parents expect it, your buddies expect it, and I guess we do too, since we've written this book to help you get in. But are you sure you really want to go?

You have many choices about what to do next year, and college is only one of them. Not everybody is ready to go to college by the end of his senior year. Maybe you worked hard in high school and want some time to yourself. Maybe you want to work on your basic skills before embarking on the rigors of college. Maybe you skipped a grade at one point and feel you're too young. Hey—maybe you're just sick of school. Whatever the reason, going to college when you're not ready for it can be a costly mistake.

If you think you need some skills, or some experience living away from home, look into a postgrad year of high school. Many prep schools offer them. Prep school courses give you more of a chance to catch up academically than do college remedial courses. A postgrad year offers you a chance to improve your record, straighten out your life, and apply to colleges as a much stronger candidate (assuming that you do the work). Junior colleges offer the same advantages: a chance to show colleges that you have changed for the better and can handle their workload.

Joining the military for a few years is another possibility. Not only will you pick up a few years' experience and gain valuable skills, but you will have a lot of financial help when you finally go to college (see Chapter Seven).

Then again, maybe you want to take a year off entirely, perhaps to see something of the world or to get work experience. If you are not sure why you are going to college, staying away for a year gives you some time to think things over.

Of course, taking a year off has its downside, too. You fall a year behind your classmates. You could wind up wasting the entire year (but then, you might have wasted your first year at college, too). Applying next year may be a hassle, especially if you don't take care of all the red tape senior year. If you don't, you will have to track down old teachers to write recommendations and have to take standardized tests a year after you stop going to classes.

So if you plan to take next year off, we strongly recommend that you apply to college *now,* and defer the starting date only after you're admitted. Take your tests, collect your recommendations, and explore your college choices now. Almost all colleges will allow you to defer if you write them with your reasons and give them proper notice (usually by May 1).

Colleges send out their decisions on April 14. If you are accepted to the college of your choice, you can use the last two weeks of April to decide whether or not you want to defer for a year. You'd be surprised how much an acceptance can change your thinking! If you don't get in anywhere, you can always reapply next year—even to the same schools (colleges admire tenacity).

We want you to go to college. You'll like it. You'll learn a lot. You'll develop social skills. When you're not studying hard it's a blast. But not everyone goes to college immediately. Don't feel pressured into it. Four years in college is too much time, too much effort, and too much money for you to be anything less than enthusiastic about going.

CHAPTER 2

TEST SCORES

"At our school SATs are so overemphasized. We took the PSAT
in tenth and eleventh, then the
SAT in eleventh and twelfth. If
I see another No. 2 pencil I'm
going to jump out the window."

I f you stood on a street corner and asked people to say the first thing that popped into their minds when you said "applying to college," a lot of them would probably answer, "SATs!" The Scholastic Aptitude Test, sponsored by the College Entrance Examination Board (College Board) and published by the Educational Testing Service (ETS), symbolizes the entire admissions process for many people. The same is true, to a lesser extent, of the ACT, a college admissions test published by a company called the American College Testing Program. (We're going to spend most of our time in this chapter talking about the SAT, which is the main standardized test required by most truly selective schools. We'll tell you more about the ACT later, and also about Achievement tests.)

How important are SATs? The answer to this question is complex. Unfortunately, most people treat the question as though it were simple. As a result, most of the information available about these tests is inaccurate. Much of the advice given to students about them is actually wrong.

HERE'S AN EXAMPLE OF WHAT WE MEAN

It's College Night at your high school, and you and your parents are attending a question-and-answer session with an admissions officer from an Ivy League university that you want to attend. Your mother raises her hand and asks if a student's SAT scores aren't the most important part of his application.

"The importance of the SAT in college admissions is greatly exaggerated," says the admissions officer. "It's one factor—*one* factor. It's not the most important factor; it's not even the *second* most important factor. I wish our applicants would spend more time worrying about their schoolwork and less time worrying about their scores on multiple-choice tests."

This sounds reasonable and reassuring. Your mother thinks, "Good, his scores don't matter." You think, "Great, I can blow off the test." Your school's guidance counselor thinks, "Wonderful, I can tell my students not to worry so much about the SAT."

But the very next day, the admissions officer goes back to his campus and resumes wading through applications.

"What do you think of X?" asks one of his colleagues, referring to a candidate they're considering.

"Good scores, nice grades. The Achievements jump around, though."

They discuss some other cases.

"That low verbal worries me . . . her TSWE score makes me wonder who wrote her essay . . . his grades are good, but the SATs are so much better I wonder if he's lazy . . . Good grades, mediocre scores—a classic overachiever."

And so on. The admissions officer wasn't lying on College Night when he said he thought the SAT was overemphasized. He just didn't realize that he was one of the people who overemphasized it.

SAT MYTHOLOGY

The story about the admissions officer illustrates an extremely important fact about standardized admissions tests: What people say about the tests very often bears little resemblance to reality. Even at schools that claim not to pay much attention to SATs, test scores are a constant topic of conversation.

Many myths have arisen about the SAT and similar tests. If you want to be a successful college candidate, you're going to have to learn to untangle fact from fiction.

WHAT, EXACTLY, IS THE SAT?

The SAT (Scholastic Aptitude Test) is a three-hour, multiple-choice test divided into six thirty-minute sections (not necessarily in this order):

1. a 45-question verbal section
2. a 40-question verbal section
3. a 25-question Test of Standard Written English
4. a 25-question math section
5. a 35-question math section
6. an experimental section

Only the two verbal sections and the two math sections count toward your SAT score. Scores on the Test of Standard Written English (TSWE) are supposed to be used only to place students in appropriate courses *after* they've been admitted to college, but in fact most admissions offices use them in making admissions decisions. (We'll tell you more about this later.) The experimental section of your SAT may look like a verbal section, a math section, or a TSWE, but it won't be scored; the test's publisher uses it to try out new SAT questions and to determine whether the test you are taking is harder or easier than ones that have been given in the past.

WHERE DOES THE SAT COME FROM?

The SAT is published by the Educational Testing Service (ETS) under the sponsorship of the College Entrance Examination Board (College Board). ETS and the College Board are not government agencies, as many people believe. Nor do they have any connection with Princeton University, as many other people believe. They are private companies that make money by selling tests. ETS sells not only the SAT but also about 500 other tests, including ones for CIA agents, golf pros, travel agents, fire fighters, and barbers.

WHO WRITES THE SAT?

Many people believe that SAT questions are written by famous college professors or experts on secondary education. This is not true. Virtually all questions are written by ordinary company employees or by college students and others hired part-time from outside ETS. Sometimes the questions are even written by teenagers. The daughter of an ETS vice president spent the summer after she graduated from high school writing questions for ETS tests.

WHAT DOES THE SAT MEASURE?

If you're like most high school students, you think of the SAT as a test of how smart you are. If you score 800 on the verbal you'll probably think of yourself as a "genius"; if you score 200 you may think of yourself as an "idiot." You may even think of an SAT score as a permanent label, like your Social Security number. ETS encourages you to think this way by telling you that the test measures aptitude—"capacity for learning"—and by claiming that you cannot improve your score through special preparation.

Students sometimes come to us depressed about their PSAT scores. They'd always thought of themselves as reasonably smart; now they're bummed out because ETS has branded them as "dumb." Their entire self-image has been deflated by a two-digit number on a piece of paper.

This shouldn't happen.

THE SCHOLASTIC APTITUDE TEST IS NOT A TEST OF SCHOLASTIC APTITUDE

The SAT isn't a test of how smart you are. It isn't a test of your "scholastic aptitude." It's simply a test of how good you are at taking ETS tests. Princeton Review students improve their SAT scores by an *average* of 150 points on the two halves of the test combined. (We'll tell you more about improving your SAT scores later.) Our students aren't any *smarter* when they finish taking our course; they're just better at taking the SAT.

One of the most important things we teach our students is not to be intimidated by the SAT. When they leave us, they think of the SAT as a game, not a life-or-death test. They no longer brag about high scores or have nightmares about low ones. They see the test for what it is: a bad joke played on more than a million kids a year by a bunch of bureaucrats in New Jersey.

WHAT DO ADMISSIONS OFFICERS THINK ABOUT THE SAT?

No matter what they say on College Night, virtually all admissions officers think of the SAT as a test of how "smart" you are. They may believe that the test is flawed, they may believe that

31

there are better measures of preparation for college (there are) —but they still think of the SAT as a measure of your intelligence. If you are an A student but have mediocre SAT scores, they'll call you an "overachiever," not an "undertester." Even college admissions officers who claim not to believe in the SAT have a powerful tendency to believe SAT scores when they see them. This tendency isn't based on past experience with real students; it's based on a nearly universal tendency to believe that numbers—any numbers—are "real" and "scientific." When admissions officers juggle numbers around, they feel that they're making objective decisions. The scores are a powerful crutch. An admissions officer once told us, "I need the numbers, and I don't care where they come from." He said he was joking—but he wasn't completely.

Some admissions officers say they don't even look at SAT scores except in certain special instances—such as when they don't have enough information about a particular applicant's high school. But this is almost never true. If your SAT scores are anywhere in your application folder (they might be on your high school transcript or in a letter from your principal in addition to being in ETS's score report), the people who read your application will look at them and be influenced by them, even if they have to peek. This is simply human nature.

THIS IS EVEN TRUE AT BOWDOIN AND BATES

Bowdoin and Bates, two fine liberal arts colleges in Maine, don't require their applicants to submit SAT scores. Does this mean they think the SAT is for the birds? Yes and no. Both colleges discovered that they didn't need the SAT to help them find good students. "We probably get a higher proportion of able students who have proven themselves to everyone but the College Board," said a spokesman for Bowdoin. Both colleges say the SAT is flawed. But admissions officers at both colleges are still affected by human nature. When they see low SAT scores in an applicant's folder, they can't help wondering, "Is this kid stupid?"

If you plan to apply to Bowdoin or Bates and if you did

poorly on the SAT, for heaven's sake don't mention your low SAT scores in your application. If you have an interview with an admissions officer, don't say, "I'm sure glad you dropped your SAT requirement, because I got a 350 on the verbal." Bowdoin's admissions officers will probably *assume* that you didn't do very well on the SAT if you don't submit your scores, but assuming is different from knowing. Don't give them a reason to doubt that you can make the grade.

The decisions at Bowdoin and Bates to drop the SAT were opposed by many faculty members who took the claims of the College Board at face value and believed the SAT was a good measure of "intelligence." Many of these faculty members still feel that way, and their opinions can put pressure, both directly and indirectly, on admissions committees. To talk about how poorly you did on the SAT is to risk making yourself seem undesirable as a candidate. Keep your scores to yourself.

WHAT ABOUT COLLEGES THAT REQUIRE SATS?

If the admissions officers at Bowdoin and Bates think about SAT scores, you can imagine how much difference your scores can make at other selective colleges. If your SAT scores are anywhere in your application folder (and if you took the test, they probably will be), someone is going to see them and be affected by them one way or the other. "The first thing I look for is the scores," an admissions officer told us.

DON'T PANIC

Before you panic, keep in mind that the psychological importance of SAT scores in the minds of college admissions officers doesn't always work against you. In addition to being the most conspicuous item of information in your folder, your SAT scores are also the easiest to change in a short period of time. There's nothing you can do about the grades you have already earned. There's nothing you can do about all the extracurricular activities you never took part in. There's nothing you can do about the time you wrecked the principal's car. But you *can* raise your SAT scores in the space of just a few months.

WHOM DO YOU BELIEVE?

ETS and the College Board have claimed for decades that SAT scores can't be improved significantly through coaching. They even have statistics to support their claim. But the Princeton Review has proved conclusively that ETS and the College Board are wrong. You can learn to do better on the SAT in precisely the same way you would learn to do better in your chemistry class: by learning the material on which you are going to be tested.

If your teacher gave you a D on a chemistry test, what would you do? You'd probably say to yourself, "I should have worked harder," or "I could have done better if I'd studied more." This is exactly the attitude you should have about the SAT. If you were disappointed by your score on the PSAT, you shouldn't think "I'm stupid"; you should think, "I need to get better at taking this test."

HOW CAN I GET BETTER AT TAKING THE SAT?

Naturally, we'd be thrilled if you signed up to take our course at one of the Princeton Review schools in dozens of American cities. We'd also be overjoyed if you bought our best-selling book, *Cracking the System: The SAT* (New York: Villard Books, 1986, $9.95). The book is available in bookstores everywhere. It contains techniques and inside information we teach in our schools. It even has a mail-in diagnostic test that we can grade and analyze on our computers. That's what we do for the students in our courses. Reading our analyses helps our students improve their scores by learning where they make mistakes— especially the mistakes they made over and over again. One of the things we strongly believe is that there are no "careless mistakes." Every mistake has a cause, and every cause can be dealt with if a student is willing to address it directly.

Our coaching course is very different from others. Our classes are small (eight to twelve students) and they're based on shared ability. Each student receives personal attention. When a student doesn't understand something in class, we work with him or her in even smaller groups, and then in one-on-one tutoring. Our teachers are sharp and enthusiastic. They did well on their SATs and graduated recently from top colleges. You'd like them.

Finally, we do our homework. Every year, we spend hundreds of thousands of dollars writing, improving, and updating our course materials. There are some coaches out there whose only research is buying our book.

ARE OTHER COACHING COURSES ANY GOOD?

That depends. There are some good coaches out there, but there are also lots and lots of bad ones. Well-meaning but mis-informed guidance counselors spread an enormous quantity of misinformation about the SAT every year.

A good way to tell whether SAT coaches know what they're talking about is to ask them whether you should guess on the test. If the coach says "no," you can be sure that he or she doesn't know what he's talking about. Intelligent guessing is one of the keys to doing better on the SAT. It's a topic on which we focus a lot of attention in our school and in our book.

Some coaches will tell you that you should only guess on the SAT if you can eliminate three answer choices. This is also wrong. If you are able to eliminate just one choice on an SAT question, you will be most likely to improve your score by guess-ing randomly among the remaining choices. Most students don't guess enough on the SAT, and the ones who do guess usually don't do it effectively.

Some students receive so much conflicting information about the SAT that they don't know what to think. One of our best students (her scores went up more than 250 points after taking our course) told us about the experience she had had before she came to us. "Every one of my teachers told us something different," she said. "My math teacher said we should never guess, because we'd lose points if we did, and that we should never go back and change an answer. My English teacher said we could guess, but only if we had narrowed it down to two possible choices. She also said we should double-check our work. My guidance counselor said we should always pick choice C when we guessed. It was insane."

Getting a lot of conflicting advice like this can be doubly damaging: It can confuse you as you prepare for the test and it can make you freeze up when you're actually taking it. If you sit there in the test center trying to decide whether or not to guess, while the clock ticks and your pencil trembles in your hand, you'll lose points unnecessarily.

WHAT DO COLLEGES THINK ABOUT COACHING?

College admissions officers have peculiar feelings about coaching. Most admissions officers nowadays do believe that coaching can improve SAT scores. At the same time, though, they believe that the SAT is a good measure of preparation for college. As a result, they tend to look down on students whose scores they suspect of having been raised through coaching. This means that if you take a coaching course, you shouldn't say so in your interview. If one of your college applications asks you how you spent your summer vacation, for goodness' sake don't say you spent it with Stanley Kaplan.

Coaching puts students in a double bind. You'd probably be crazy not to prepare for the test. But if you prepare for the test, you'll probably have to pretend you didn't. If people were rational about the SAT, this problem wouldn't exist. But people are most definitely not rational about the SAT, and they give no indication that they are going to *become* rational any time in the foreseeable future.

Many college admissions officers actually deduct points from the SAT scores of students they assume have been coached for the test. If you attend a fancy private school in New York City, Ivy League admissions officers will probably take it for granted that you took a coaching course. You should keep this in mind as you try to decide whether or not to take one.

WHEN DO I START?

Admissions officers often assume you've been coached if your scores rise by more than a hundred points or so between the first and second times you take the test, or between the time you take the PSAT and the time you take the SAT. What this means is that the earlier you begin preparing for the SAT, the better off you're going to be. You'll be better off if you get your scores up before any numbers go into your permanent record.

Some people advise taking a coaching course before PSATs. We don't agree. The admissions testing game is absurd enough as it is. There's no need to extend the frenzy.

Some students need to do more than this in preparation for the PSAT, however. Many high schools include PSAT scores on their transcripts (they shouldn't). Admissions officers say they see the PSAT scores of about half their applicants. These scores can affect your chances. Because they can, you must at least familiarize yourself with the test before you take it. Look at the sample test and be sure you understand the question types. You might even consider taking a course.

If standardized tests make you frantic, you need to learn enough about the test to calm your fears. The more you know, the less intimidated you'll be. You should also consider preparing for the test if you think you have a chance at winning a National Merit Scholarship.

PREPARING FOR THE SAT

Here's a list of some of the things you need to do before you take the SAT:

1. KNOW THE TIMETABLE

The SAT is given at different times during the year. If you go to a school with a strong college preparatory program, your guidance counselor will probably make certain that you don't miss any deadlines. If your school's guidance department is weak or understaffed, you need to take things into your own hands. Get a registration form from your guidance office in the first semester of your junior year. Along with the application you should be given a booklet called *Taking the SAT,* which contains a sample test. If you can't afford the registration fee, it will be waived. *Don't be afraid to ask for a fee waiver; too many students skip the test because they think they can't afford the fee. ETS and the College Board never spend more than a tiny fraction of the money they set aside each year for fees for students who can't pay.*

Be sure you pay attention to deadlines. ETS and the College Board charge huge penalty fees for students who sign up late or take the test on a stand-by basis. When you receive your admission ticket to the test, be sure you look carefully at the test center to which you have been assigned. Don't assume that it will automatically be your own high school. If you show up at the wrong location on Saturday morning, you could either miss the test entirely or have to pay a penalty fee.

Making a mistake like this can happen to anyone who isn't careful. It even happened to one of our teachers. "When I was in high school I signed up for the SAT and the Achievements at the same time. The SAT was first, and I took it at a big high school across town. I just assumed that the Achievements would be given at the same place. I never even looked at my ticket. Then, that morning, I stood in the cold for an hour with two other guys. It never even occurred to me that I was standing in the wrong place until after it was too late. I just kept thinking, How strange—only three people signed up to take the test."

2. PRACTICE WITH REAL SATs

One of the best ways to learn about the SAT is to practice on real tests. The College Board publishes a collection of real tests called *10 SATs* (New York: College Entrance Examination Board, 1986, second edition, $8.95). It's usually available in bookstores. You can also order it, and other collections of tests, from the College Board. For more information, write to:

College Board Publications
Box 886
New York, NY 10101

3. DON'T PAY ATTENTION TO OTHER SAT BOOKS

Most SAT-preparation books (not including ours, of course) don't have much to do with the real test. Some were written years ago by "experts" who had little specific information to offer about real SATs. (ETS only started releasing SATs in 1980.) Sometimes following the advice in popular SAT guides can actually *hurt* your scores. One of the best-selling SAT books contains a strategy for solving SAT analogies that actually leads students to *incorrect* answers. Another includes drills for an item type that hasn't been used on the SAT in sixty years. The same is true of most computerized coaching programs. We have yet to see one of these that isn't a waste of money.

4. WORK ON YOUR VOCABULARY

The verbal SAT is little more than a vocabulary test. Students with big vocabularies almost invariably earn high verbal SAT scores; students with small vocabularies almost invariably earn low ones.

In order to do well on the verbal SAT, you need to improve your vocabulary. This takes time, so start immediately. Don't try to do it by memorizing the dictionary; you'll never get past the first page, and you won't learn any words that will help you on the test.

You also shouldn't try to prepare for the verbal SAT by studying the word lists in most SAT-preparation books. These lists often contain hundreds of words that have never been tested, and never will be tested, on the SAT. Most of the words in the popular coaching books are just *too hard* to be used on real SATs. *Cracking the System: The SAT,* on the other hand, contains a word list called the Hit Parade, which consists of the actual words tested most frequently on the SAT. (The top three words are *indifferent, apathy,* and *obscure,* in case you were wondering.) Our list contains just 252 words. We used a computer

39

to help us put it together. You can do the same thing we did by studying published SATs.

The best way to improve your vocabulary is to read widely. This will not only help you on the SAT but will also make you a smarter and more interesting person.

5. TAKE A MATH COURSE

Many schools permit their students to stop taking math courses in eleventh grade. Students who aren't currently taking math courses do worse on the math SAT than students who are. Even (or especially) if you struggle in math, you should consider signing up for more math at least for junior year. If you haven't taken Algebra II already, take it. If you have taken Algebra II, see if your school offers something like Pre-Calculus, College Math, or Advanced Algebra—some course for students who want to keep taking math but don't want to take the big plunge into calculus. (Incidentally, there's no trigonometry or calculus on the SAT—just arithmetic, geometry, and algebra.)

6. DON'T GO TO BED AT SEVEN

Some guidance counselors tell their students to get a lot of sleep the night before the SAT. This probably isn't a good idea. If you aren't used to sleeping twelve hours a night, doing so will just make you feel groggy.

A much better idea is to get up early each morning for the entire week before the test and do your homework before school. This will get your brain accustomed to functioning at that hour of the morning. You want to be sharp at test time.

ON THE DAY OF THE TEST AND BEYOND

1. HAVE PROPER IDENTIFICATION

You are supposed to take identification to your test center. ETS's definition of acceptable ID is "Any official document bearing the candidate's name and photograph, or name and description (driver's license, school ID, or current passport)."

If you find yourself at the test center with *unacceptable* ID (one with name and signature only), you *should* be admitted anyway. According to the ETS rule book, you should be asked to fill out an identification verification form and then allowed to take the test. If you really do turn out to be yourself, your scores will count.

If you arrive without any identification at all, a literal-minded supervisor could turn you away. One of our students got around this problem in a creative way. When the proctor told her she couldn't take the test, she simply took out a blank sheet of paper, wrote out a brief description of herself, and signed it.

"That is *not* acceptable identification," the proctor said.

"I know," said the student. "But the rules say students with unacceptable ID can take the test and supply real ID later."

She was allowed to take the test. Another possibility is to ask permission to call home and have someone drop off your driver's license while you're taking the test. That way you can have everything cleared up before you leave.

2. HAVE ENOUGH NO. 2 PENCILS

The only outside materials you are allowed to use on the test are No. 2 pencils (take four of them, all sharp) and a wristwatch (an absolute necessity). Digital watches are best. If you have a calculator watch, be prepared to have it confiscated. Proctors should also confiscate other calculators, pocket dictionaries, word lists, portable computers, and the like, although they often fail to do this. Proctors have also occasionally confiscated stopwatches and travel clocks. Technically, you should be permitted to use these, but you can never tell with some proctors. Take a watch and avoid the hassles.

3. TAKE BRAIN FOOD

Some proctors allow students to bring food into the test room; others don't. Take a soda and a candy bar with you and see what happens. If you open them quietly and don't flaunt them, they probably won't be confiscated. Save them until you're about halfway through the test. Remember that it takes about ten minutes for sugar to work its way to your tired brain. If the proctor yells at you, surrender them cheerfully and continue with the test.

Counting the time you spend sitting or standing around and the time your proctor spends reading instructions, you'll probably end up spending four or five hours at the test center. Eat a light breakfast before you go, but don't eat a big heavy meal that will make you feel sleepy for the first hour of the test.

4. GET COMFORTABLE

You are going to be sitting in the same place for more than three hours, so make sure your desk isn't broken or unusually uncomfortable. If you are left-handed, ask for a left-handed desk. (The center may not have one, but it won't hurt to ask.) If the sun is in your eyes, ask to move. If the room is too dark, ask someone to turn on the lights. Don't hesitate to speak up. Some proctors just don't know what they're doing. If you know you're in the right, stick to your guns or to ask to speak to the supervisor. (The proctor is the person in charge of your room; the supervisor is the person in charge of the entire test center.)

5. MAKE SURE YOUR BOOKLET IS COMPLETE

Before you start the test, make sure your booklet is complete. You can quickly turn through all the pages without reading them. Booklets sometimes contain printing errors that make some pages impossible to read. Find out ahead of time and demand a new booklet if yours is defective. Don't, however, read questions or give the proctor the impression that you've started the test early. Also, check your answer sheet to make sure it isn't flawed.

6. YOU DESERVE A BREAK

You should get a five-minute break after the first hour of the test. Ask for it if your proctor doesn't give it to you. You should be allowed to go to the bathroom at this time. You should also be allowed to take a one-minute break at your desk at the end of the second hour. The breaks are a very good idea. They let you clear your head. Insist on them.

7. DON'T CANCEL YOUR SCORES UNLESS ...

ETS allows you to cancel your SAT scores. Unfortunately, you can no longer cancel only your math, verbal, or TSWE score—

it's all or nothing. You can cancel scores at the test center by asking your proctor for a "Cancellation Request Form." If you decide to cancel later on, you can do so by sending a telegram to ETS. You must do this before the Wednesday following the test.

We recommend that you *not* cancel your scores unless you know you made so many errors, or left out so many questions, that your score will be unacceptably low. Don't cancel your scores because you have a bad feeling—students frequently have an exaggerated sense of how many mistakes they made, and it's possible you did much better than you realize.

8. CHECK YOUR ANSWER SHEET

Make sure you darken all your responses before the test is over. At the same time, erase any extraneous marks on the answer sheet. Seriously: A stray mark in the margin of your answer sheet can result in correct responses being marked wrong.

9. CHECK UP ON ETS

Send away for ETS's Question and Answer Service. It costs a little money, but it's worth it. You'll get back a copy of your answer sheet, a test booklet, and an answer key. Check your answers against the key and complain if you think you've been misscored. (Don't throw away the test booklet you receive from the Question and Answer Service. If you're planning to take the SAT again, save it for practice. If not, give it to your guidance counselor or school library.)

10. CALL US

If you have a problem with your test, call the Princeton Review at 1–800–JBLOGGS. ETS is unbelievably slow about looking into complaints. They are not sympathetic to student concerns. We are.

IS ONCE ENOUGH? IS THREE TIMES TOO MANY?

How many times you should take the SAT is a good question to which there is no simple answer. Most high school students should probably take it twice, once in the spring of their junior year and once in the fall of their senior year. If you go to a college preparatory high school, this is probably what you will be encouraged to do by your guidance counselor. Most students' scores go up the second time they take the test (although the higher your score is the first time, the less likely it will be to go up the second). You probably should *not* take the SAT three or more times. If you take the test repeatedly, admissions officers will think you are the testing equivalent of a grade-grubber. Applicants who appear pushy are always at a disadvantage, and applicants who take the SAT more than twice usually appear pushy.

There are exceptions to these general guidelines, however. These are spelled out below:

1. IF YOU ARE APPLYING TO A STATE UNIVERSITY

Many state colleges and universities use fairly strict formulas to determine who will be admitted and who will be rejected. For example, you can qualify for admission to the University of California system simply by scoring at least 1100 (math and verbal combined) on the SAT or 26 (composite). (You also have to score a total of 1650 or higher on three Achievement tests, with no single score below 500). There are a couple of other requirements, but there is no limitation on the number of times you can take the tests. Practice, get help, and keep trying.

(Keep in mind that scoring 1100 guarantees you admission to the California *system*, not to a particular school. High-powered schools like Berkeley are more selective and thus harder to get into, especially if you are applying from out of state.)

2. IF YOU ARE A TERRIBLE TEST-TAKER

If you always do miserably on standardized tests (say, between 200 and 400 on each half of the SAT), and if you have gotten help from a coach but still not improved, and if your grades are pretty good—you might consider taking the SAT only once. One set of terrible scores doesn't look as decisive as two. If you score 310 on the verbal the first time, scoring 320 the second time isn't going to make you a more attractive college candidate. If you have only one set of scores in your record, you will at least leave open the possibility that your performance was a fluke. (If you have a learning disability or perceptual problem that limits your performance on the test, check with your counselor or with the College Board. Special arrangements can be made for students who need them.)

3. IF YOU DID EXTREMELY WELL THE FIRST TIME

If you scored above 700 on both halves of the SAT the first time you took it, why take it again and run the risk of scoring 600's? Keep in mind that students who score above 1100 or so the first time they take the SAT are most likely to do *a little worse* the second time they take it. Don't be greedy.

4. IF YOU CAN WIN MONEY

Some colleges pay generous scholarships based on nothing more than a student's SAT scores. If you're close to the cutoff, go for it.

THE TEST OF STANDARD WRITTEN ENGLISH

A few years ago, ETS and the College Board added a new thirty-minute section to the SAT called the Test of Standard Written English (TSWE). The TSWE is almost exactly like part of the English Composition Achievement Test. It is supposed to be used by colleges to place the students they admit in appropriate courses. It is not supposed to be used in making admissions decisions.

However, TSWE scores are reported right alongside your SAT scores, and all colleges use them in making admissions decisions. Colleges generally use TSWE scores as an indication of your "writing ability." This is absurd, but they do it anyway. If you blow off the TSWE because you think it doesn't count, an admissions officer may decide, say, that somebody smarter than you must have written that wonderful essay in your application.

The TSWE is a silly test, but doing well on it is an easy way to earn some points with admissions officers. Don't rush through it.

ACHIEVEMENT TESTS

Most selective colleges require you to take one or more Achievement tests in addition to the SAT. There are fourteen different Achievement tests in thirteen different subjects. Like the SAT, they are written by ETS under the sponsorship of the College Board.

Admissions officers generally believe that the SAT measures what you are capable of doing while the Achievements measure what you have actually done. If you do better on the verbal SAT than on the English Composition Achievement, you will be said to be an "underachiever."

This is entirely unfounded. The SAT and the Achievements are almost exactly the same kinds of tests, and they test almost exactly the same kinds of skills. As with the SAT, the best preparation for the Achievements is a thorough grounding in test-taking skills and an understanding of how the test-makers think.

Here are a few other points to keep in mind about the Achievements:

1. SHOP AROUND

Colleges that require Achievements usually suggest that you take three: Math I or Math II, English Composition, and one other test of your own choosing.

Math II isn't necessarily harder than Math I. Which you should take depends on which math classes you've taken in school. If you're a junior in pre-calculus, you've studied the material tested in Math II more recently than the material tested in Math I. You may thus find the more "advanced" test to be easier. Take sample tests to be sure. (You can see samples of all fourteen Achievement tests in a book called *The College Board Achievement Tests*, published by the College Board and sold in bookstores [New York: College Entrance Examination Board, 1986, second edition, $11.95.])

If the choice of test is left up to you, shop around. Some of the tests are much easier than others. The physics test, for example, is very hard, because most of the top science students in the country take physics; the biology test is generally said to be the easiest; the chemistry test is graded on a generous curve. If you do well in English class—and especially if you do well on multiple-choice reading comprehension questions—you will probably do well, or even extremely well, on the English literature test. (This test, which consists solely of reading comprehension questions, is not to be confused with the English composition test. The English literature test is usually overlooked, but many students say it's the easiest Achievement there is.) Students who have taken foreign languages usually find the foreign language Achievements easy. Don't assume that any of the Achievements are hard. Check them out before you decide, and then take as many as you feel you can do well on.

Similarly, you should never take an Achievement test that you won't do well on (unless it's required). To see why, consider these two students and their Achievement records:

Joe B.		*Joe A.*	
Math I	720	Math I	720
Eng. Comp.	540	Eng. Comp.	540
Biology	610	Biology	610
French	500		
U.S. History	420		

Joe B. did as well as Joe A. on math, English, and biology. In addition, he took two more tests. So who has the better record? Joe A. does. Joe B. has given colleges two more reasons to reject him—two uninspiring scores. Three good scores is all anyone needs.

You aren't trying on hats when you take Achievements. You should take only those tests on which you are certain to do well. Colleges will see your scores on every test you take, not just the three that may be required. For this reason, you should never take a few Achievements "just for practice," unless you are careful to cancel your scores. We knew of a student who, in order to get a feel for college entrance tests, took the tests in Hebrew

47

and physics, two subjects in which he was entirely ignorant. Instead of gaining experience, he blotted his record with two terrible scores.

2. DON'T ACT LIKE A NERD

If you're a dyed-in-the-wool pre-med, take something besides math and science Achievements if possible. If you take Math II, Physics, and Chemistry, an admissions officer may decide you're a basket case. Some guides say it doesn't matter which Achievements you take, but it can. Doing well on a variety of Achievement tests is a relatively easy way to look like a broadly accomplished person.

3. PARLEZ-VOUS FRANÇAIS?

If you spent your first sixteen years living in Paris, by all means take the French Achievement. It will help your average score.

4. THERE ARE TWO ENGLISH COMPOSITION TESTS

ETS and the College Board offer two tests in English composition. One consists entirely of multiple-choice questions; one consists of multiple-choice questions plus a short essay. The essay version of the test is offered only in December. Some schools require it; most give you a choice.

Which should you choose? That depends on your test-taking skills. We have had a great deal of success coaching students for both versions of the test. Even students who can't write well can do extremely well on the essay version. Before making your decision, take sample versions of both tests.

5. HIGH ACHIEVEMENTS CAN REDEEM LOWER SATs

Many college admissions officers are going through a phase of preferring Achievement tests to SATs. Some colleges even give more weight to Achievement scores than they do to SATs.

THE ACT

The ACT is the college admissions test of the American College Testing Program. It is the SAT's one big competitor. About a million and a quarter students take the SAT every year; about three quarters of a million take the ACT. Many people believe that the ACT is more "achievement"-oriented than the SAT is, but this claim is groundless. For all practical purposes, the ACT and the SAT are the same kind of test. (It is true, however, that some people consistently do better on one test than on the other.)

Some colleges give you the choice of taking either the ACT or the SAT. If you're a mediocre test-taker and have no reason for taking one test instead of the other, you might consider taking the ACT instead of the SAT. The reason is that ACT scores don't have the same emotional impact on people as SAT scores.

Though the ACT is very widely used, it is required by only a very few truly selective schools. Most of the colleges that require the ACT have extremely low rejection rates. Before you get all worked up about having to take the ACT, make certain that you aren't worrying unnecessarily.

PSAT AND PRA

The PSAT is the Preliminary Scholastic Aptitude Test. It was introduced years ago to give students practice with an ETS test before they were required to take the SAT. In 1973, ETS tied the PSAT to the National Merit Scholarship. Now, instead of being merely a "practice" SAT, the PSAT became a crucial test for many students. More and more of them started preparing for it. Responding to students' anxiety, some high schools started administering a practice PSAT at the start of the sophomore year. Currently more than twenty percent of high schools do this. Further, as the distinction between the PSAT and SAT has blurred, an increasing number of high schools have begun including PSAT scores from both sophomore and junior years on students' transcripts, raising student anxieties even more. Instead of allaying fears, the PSAT has compounded them. Beginning in academic year 1987, the American College Testing Program will begin publishing a similar test.

We at the Princeton Review wish that scholarship committees would tie their awards to the SAT, ACT, or even AP tests instead. Using what is supposed to be a practice test for scholarship awards only promotes confusion and tension. A true practice test should be for student and counselor use only.

This is why the Princeton Review has introduced a new practice test of its own—the Princeton Review Assessment (PRA). Our test includes questions similar to those on the SAT and ACT and offers students a chance to find out how they can expect to perform on each of those tests. Our score reports tell students which test will best represent them. They also provide full diagnostic analyses of students' responses, highlighting each student's strengths and weaknesses. Ask your guidance counselor about it.

If the PRA isn't offered at your school yet, ask your guidance counselor to get in touch with us at 1-800-333-0369. Our mailing address is:

> The Princeton Review
> Attn: PRA
> 606 Columbus Avenue
> New York, NY 10024

QUESTIONS AND ANSWERS

Don't colleges look only at your best SAT scores?

Different people will tell you different things about how colleges use SAT scores: They use only the best ones, they use only the worst ones, they use only the most recent ones, they use only the average of all of them, and so on. For the most part, none of this is true. Admissions officers usually end up seeing all of your SAT scores. If there's a low score in there, it will be noticed even if the school has a "policy" of using only the best score. Lower scores that stand out can also make colleges suspicious of your high scores.

Some students think they should take the SAT once for practice, just to get the feel of it, and then take it again later for real and have those scores reported. If you do this, keep in mind that unless you cancel those first "practice" scores before the

Wednesday after you take the test, your first scores will appear on the score reports ETS sends out after you take the test a second time. Once your scores are in ETS's records, there's almost nothing you can do to get rid of them.

If my SAT scores are low, should I explain in my essay?

Never, never, *never* try to explain away low SAT scores. Admissions officers have heard every excuse you could ever come up with, and they don't believe any of them. Talking about bad SAT scores only draws attention to them. (Incidentally, talking about good SAT scores reduces their value. If you did well on the SAT, don't brag about it. Everyone will notice without any help from you.)

Should my guidance counselor write a letter explaining my low SAT scores?

No, unless there is a real, certified, absolute, undeniable, incontrovertible excuse for how poorly you did. There are only about three such excuses, and they all involve physical illnesses or tragic accidents. *Don't* let your guidance counselor write a letter simply saying that you're smarter than your SAT scores indicate or that you freeze up on standardized tests.

Should I fill out the Student Descriptive Questionnaire?

When you sign up for the SAT, you'll be offered a chance to answer a lot of questions about your achievements, interests, goals, and family situation. We recommend that you *not* fill out this form.

There are several reasons. First, it's a bad idea in college admissions to answer questions you haven't been asked. If the college of your dreams wants to know how many of your brothers and sisters are in college, let it ask you. Everything you write down in the SDQ will be seen by the colleges to which you apply. If you say in it that you're planning to be a pre-med, and the colleges to which you've applied don't want any more premeds, you'll be out of luck. You also don't necessarily want to present yourself in the same way to every college to which you apply.

The SDQ is a big business for ETS and the College Board (they sell lists of names to military recruiters, among others) and a marketing tool for colleges. It doesn't help students. Don't waste your time; don't fill it out.

What's the difference between a 610 and a 590?

More than twenty points. People are funny. They'll buy something for $99.99 that they would never buy for $100, even though there's only a penny's difference in the price. Admissions officers are the same way about SAT scores. The *real* difference between a 610 and a 590 is only one or two questions, but most admissions officers will view a 610 as a significantly better prospect than a 590 even though they view a 610 and a 630 as being about the same. If you come close to one of the hundred-point plateaus the first time you take the test, get some practice and take it again.

Do Ivy League colleges have minimum SAT requirements?

Most selective colleges say they don't have minimum SAT requirements, but in effect all of them do. The cutoff may be fairly informal, but it's still real. If you don't score above that cutoff (whatever it is) you won't have a chance.

Admissions officers at very selective colleges will often try to reassure applicants by pointing out, say, how many students they admit who have verbal scores below 550. But if you look carefully at who these students are, you usually discover that virtually all of them are minorities, athletes, children of alumni, or other special cases.

There's no way to know what the effective cutoff is for schools in which you may be interested. Unless you are a "special case" yourself, you should keep in mind that the *true* median score for Yale, Princeton, and other highly selective schools is probably anywhere from twenty-five to one hundred points higher than the one published in the big directories.

Which is more important, the verbal or the math?

Almost all colleges care more about the verbal SAT than about the math SAT for almost all of their applicants. Ideally, of course, you want both scores to be good and reasonably close to each other. But if you have to pick (and of course you can't), the verbal is more important. (If your math scores are bad, remember not to say that you want to be a math major or have a career in the sciences.)

CHAPTER 3

GRADES AND
EXTRACURRICULAR
ACTIVITIES

*"My junior year in high school, I
signed up for a course that you
could either take pass/fail or for
a grade. I took it for a grade
because I 'needed the A.' I got a
C. Oh, well. I got into college
anyway."*

I f your SAT scores are terrible, you can probably improve them through coaching and hard work. If your grades are terrible, you're in a tight spot. Did we hear you say you're a first-semester senior?

You may be surprised to learn that much the same is true of extracurricular activities. If you've been hanging out at the video game parlor for the last three years, you're not going to help your college admissions chances very much by running out and signing up for a lot of interesting after-school activities. As with grades, long-term results are what primarily interest colleges.

If you still have a year or two left before your applications are due, we can probably help you improve your chances of being admitted to the sort of college you want to attend, and maybe help you get a better and more interesting high school experience at the same time. And if you've been earning good grades and taking part in interesting activities all along, we can help you present your record on your application so that it places you in the best possible light.

WHY GRADES MATTER

College admissions officers are interested in many things, but one of the things they're most interested in is making sure that the students they admit as freshmen won't all flunk out. All selective colleges want to fill their classes with students who are capable of doing the work. No college wants to traumatize its freshmen by throwing them into a situation they aren't equipped to handle.

Probably the best indication colleges have of how well you'll do in college is how well you've done in high school. Even the College Board and ETS admit that high school grades are better predictors of college success than SAT scores. As a result, colleges pay a lot of attention to the grades you've earned since ninth grade. The more successful you've been, the better your chances will be.

Each year, by the way, is more important than the last. Nothing looks better than steadily improving grades. Marks from junior and senior year are most important.

IS AN A ALWAYS AN A?

You are undoubtedly aware that different teachers at your school hand out grades in different ways. Some give A's to kids who do little more than show up every day. Others can't bring themselves to award anything higher than a B. Everybody knows stories like this. We heard about a teacher who had given extra credit to several students who helped him clean out his garage one weekend. Very unfair, of course, unless you were one of the students who got the boost.

Much the same is true of different high schools. An A from your high school may be worth a lot more, in the mind of an admissions officer, than an A from a high school across town. It may also be worth less. It all depends on your school's grading policies and on admissions officers' familiarity with those policies.

When college admissions officers sit down to wade through each year's crop of applications, one of the most important things they have to do is decide how impressed they should be by individual transcripts. If they aren't familiar with your high school already, they need to know how to interpret your grades. They do this not only by trying to understand your school's grading system, but also by evaluating the caliber of courses you've been taking.

WHAT'S WRONG WITH THE COURSES I'VE BEEN TAKING?

Maybe nothing. But you shouldn't think that the A you earned in Film Comedy is going to shine as brightly as the A your best friend earned in Advanced Chemistry. All A's are not created equal. Anybody can inflate a grade point average by taking a lot of easy electives that don't require much thought or work. You (and your parents) may enjoy seeing the A's on your report cards, but don't expect college admissions officers to be as easily impressed by your transcript. The names of the courses you took are going to be printed right there next to the grades you earned. If the courses are dopey, the A's won't matter.

IS A B IN A HARD COURSE BETTER THAN AN A IN AN EASY COURSE?

This is a question that college admissions officers and guidance counselors hear all the time. They usually answer by saying that tough, academic courses are much better than frivolous ones and that grades in tough courses are given more weight than grades in easy ones. But you should keep in mind what Stanford reminds its applicants: "Be careful not to assume that the world is divided between students who take difficult courses and get B's and the students who take easy courses and get A's. Most of our applicants are able to take difficult courses and receive A's."

Of course, not everyone wants to go to Stanford, and not everyone can make straight A's. But the general principle always applies. If you can handle the work in honors, Advanced Placement, or other accelerated courses, you should probably be taking at least a few of them. (Many schools even add points to the grade point averages of students who take these harder courses.) If it is obvious from your transcript that you are taking a lighter load than you can handle, admissions officers at selective colleges are going to wonder about your motivation. They will be especially concerned if the difficulty of your courseload drops off noticeably in eleventh grade.

On the other hand, a D in Advanced Placement history is not more impressive than a D in ceramics. It may even look worse. Don't get in over your head.

WHAT'S IN A NAME?

No matter what level you feel comfortable at, though, you should be aware of how your transcript will appear to admissions committees. Even if you can't handle accelerated work, you can at least stay away from the kinds of courses that set off alarms in the minds of admissions officers.

What kinds of courses are these? You probably know already. They're the electives you sign up for because they sound fun and easy: Children's Literature, Sailing, Hollywood Biographies, The Detective Novel, Darkroom Technique, History of Spaceflight, German Cooking, and independent study in almost anything. Courses like this began to abound in the late nineteen-sixties when students began to complain that traditional subjects weren't "relevant" to their lives. Many high school and college educators agreed at the time. The consensus has changed now, yet a lot of the old "electives" remain in high school curricula.

THE BIG TIP-OFF

One mistake a lot of students make is to fill their schedules with easy electives as soon as they've fulfilled their schools' minimum academic requirements. That's what Joe Bloggs did. His high school requires two years of science, two years of math, one year of a foreign language, two years of history, and four years of English. By the time he'd finished tenth grade, he had satisfied all of these requirements except English. He had never done well in math and science, so he didn't sign up for any math or science courses his junior year. Instead he took a pottery course and did an independent study on investing in the stock market. To satisfy his English requirement, he signed up for a course called Doonesbury, Peanuts, and Krazy Kat: The Literature of the Comics. He also took Driver Education, Phys. Ed., and Photography.

Here's what Joe's transcript looked like by the end of his junior year:

Ninth Grade	*Tenth Grade*	*Eleventh Grade*
English 9	English 10	Literature of
World History	U.S. History	Comics
Algebra I	Geometry	Independent
Earth Science	Biology	Study: Stock
Personal Hygiene	Spanish I	Market
Phys. Ed.	Phys. Ed.	Photography
		Pottery
		Driver Education
		Phys. Ed.

Never mind what Joe's grades were. The most important fact about Joe's transcript is the courses listed on it. There isn't an admissions officer in the country who wouldn't look at this transcript and think something like, "Joe decided to take a year off his junior year." Joe's college prospects will be even bleaker if he decides (as he probably will) to put together a similar schedule for his senior year.

WHAT TO DO INSTEAD

The top college candidates in the country won't have transcripts that look anything like Joe's. They'll have taken courses like AP United States History, AP English, Calculus, Chemistry, Physics, French IV, and so on. If you can handle high-powered courses like that, you ought to be taking them. In addition to increasing your attractiveness to admissions officers, you'll be getting a better education.

But even if, like Joe Bloggs, you don't feel up to taking (or can't qualify for) a lot of accelerated courses, you can at least keep your transcript from looking like it belongs to someone whose mind is on vacation. Here are some specific tips, broken down by subject area:

English: Many high schools still permit students to satisfy English requirements with phony-sounding electives like Film Animation and Psychology of Advertising. If your school offers an English course called simply "English," that's probably what you should be taking. If you can't resist taking an elective, be sure the one you sign up for sounds serious. The Novels of Dickens isn't as bad as Contemporary Fiction (generally speaking, avoid courses about writers who are still alive). Shakespeare's Tragedies and Expository Writing are better than The Films of Woody Allen and Writing for Television. The very worst English electives are the ones that have nothing to do with English, even if your school permits them to count towards an English requirement.

History: It is often somewhat easier to find history electives that sound both serious and interesting. Contemporary European History or the Russian Revolution wouldn't look bad on a transcript. Avoid courses on current events and ones that have clever names (for example, Riots and Revolutions). American history is always a good bet, and most schools offer several courses. European history is good too.

Math: Many students find math frightening and difficult. They eagerly look forward to the day when they'll finally have accumulated enough credits to be able to stop taking math courses altogether. They complain that algebra doesn't help them in their daily lives, and that it never will help them in their daily lives. Though they're probably right, they should keep in mind that math will be useful—not just for the SAT and transcript, but for majors like architecture, engineering, or any science.

If math baffles you, you don't need to sign up for Calculus, especially if you'd just earn bad grades in it anyway. Most schools do offer serious-sounding math courses—with names like Advanced Math or College Algebra—intended for students who don't want to knock themselves out in accelerated courses. You don't have to pretend that you want to be a mathematician when you grow up, but continuing with math in your transcript is a good way to keep from looking like a slacker. It's also a very good way to stay in shape for the math SAT. (Don't take a course called something like Math for the SAT, however. You'll look like one of those pushy types that admissions offices don't like. College applicants should be like politicians: ambitious without looking ambitious.)

Sciences: What we said about math courses also applies to science courses. And the closer you stick to the basic sciences (biology, chemistry, physics), the better off you'll be. Science courses in psychology, geology, astronomy, and similar subjects are less likely to seem impressive.

Foreign Languages: One year of a foreign language doesn't look much better on a transcript than no years. Two years doesn't look much better than one. No one can learn to speak and read fluently in one or two years.

Taking three or more years of *the same* foreign language is a good way to add seriousness to your transcript. (Don't make the mistake of taking one year of French, one year of Spanish, and one year of German.) A long-term commitment to a language shows not only that you don't mind studying but also that you have the gumption to stick with something over a long period of time. If you took Latin last year, stick with it.

Languages offer another admissions bonus, too. When education critics talk about the "crisis in our schools," one thing they talk about is the decline in the teaching of foreign languages. Some schools no longer offer foreign languages at all. Taking languages makes you look like one of the old-fashioned, committed students that admissions officers dream about.

Typing: One of the things our students tell us most often is that they wish they had taken typing in high school. College professors usually expect papers to be typed. If you are a poor typist, you'll waste hundreds of hours pecking out your papers over the course of your four years in college. If you don't type at all, you'll waste hundreds of dollars hiring other people to do it for you. If you plan to do any work with computers, you'll need to know how to type in order to use computer keyboards.

A typing course won't enhance your transcript. But it will make your life a lot easier after you are enrolled. Here's how one of our old students put it: "I sometimes think I spent half of my freshman year worrying about typing. If I typed my papers myself, I had to start way before the papers were due, because I was so slow. For longer papers, I usually hired typists, but that was not only expensive—it was also incredibly nerve-wracking, because sometimes it was hard to find anybody to do it. Especially if it was at the end of a term, everybody had their own papers to type. I ended up spending the summer after my freshman year taking typing lessons. It made for a boring summer, but it sure improved college."

DON'T STOP WORKING

Virtually all colleges require your high school to update your transcript with a mid-year grade report in the middle of your senior year. If you slack off during the first semester of your senior year, you can ruin your chances of being admitted to a selective college. We know a student whose early acceptance was actually withdrawn because of his poor performances during the first semester of senior year. Colleges really do care about your first-semester senior grades. Be very careful. (Actually, you have to screw up pretty badly to have an acceptance withdrawn. But you would be surprised at how many students find ways to screw up pretty badly.)

CLASS RANK

Many colleges say that class rank is more revealing than simple grade point average. (Most are interested in both.) Students who end up near the bottom of their high school classes tend to end up near the bottom of their college classes as well. The only way to move up in your class ranking (short of murdering the people ahead of you) is to earn better grades.

Some top college prep schools refuse to calculate exact class ranks because they believe a precise ranking would be misleading. At some competitive prep schools, the difference between, say, the tenth student and thirtieth student in a class of one hundred can be just a few tenths or even hundredths of a grade point. The tenth student might have a grade point average of 91.7 on a scale of 100, and the thirtieth might have an average of 90.9. The difference between those two students might be nothing more than a flunked geometry test in ninth grade.

If the grade point averages in your school are bunched up like this, be sure that your guidance counselor includes an explanatory note with your transcript (and those of other students from your school). Don't make the explanation yourself, even if the application you're filling out provides a space in which you can "explain" unusual information. If an explanation is needed, it's better to have it come from someone other than you.

GRADING SYSTEMS

The same is true if your school uses a grading system that deviates in any way from one of the standard grading systems. If an 85 is counted as an A at your school, colleges should know.

Admissions officers rely on high schools to help them understand peculiarities in the way they hand out grades. Good high schools routinely include explanations of their grading systems with the transcripts of their students. (They also include other information about the way they operate.) If your school doesn't do this, it should, especially if your school has never or has only rarely sent students to the colleges to which you are applying. Admissions officers never feel they have too much information about the high schools from which they receive applicants.

Making sure colleges have enough information is especially important if your school is in any way unusual. One high school we know about requires all its students to take a course called Interpersonal Relationships. A course with a name like that might sound like a hokey elective on your transcript; the colleges you apply to should know that you had no choice about taking it.

It would usually be ill-advised for *you* to explain your school's grading system. Just check with your guidance counselor to be sure your school is providing enough information to enable colleges to give you a fair shake.

PASS/FAIL

Never take a course pass/fail. Admissions officers don't know what to make of a "pass" on your transcript. They may count it as a C or even a D in calculating your grade point average. They will certainly decide that you were coasting when you took that course. At the very least you should never take a solid academic course pass/fail. (You may have no choice about taking some courses, like driver education and typing, pass/fail; that's not what we're talking about.)

If you go to an "experimental" high school that doesn't give grades or that gives written evaluations instead of grades, your SAT and Achievement scores are going to be given much, much more weight than they might be otherwise, and it would be to your advantage to prepare very carefully for the tests. Unfortunately, experimental high schools usually don't prepare students very well for tests like the SAT. Their curricula don't emphasize the cut-and-dried basics (like arithmetic and vocabulary) that are the heart of the SAT. Even more important, experimental schools are seldom tuned to the same unimaginative wavelength that emanates from ETS. At the Princeton Review, we regularly teach a large number of students from a high school that one of our teachers refers to as a "hippy school." The students are quite bright, but they read too much into straightforward SAT questions and their scores suffer as a result. Teaching these students is hard, because we have to show them a whole new way of thinking—the way of thinking that flourishes at ETS. Then, after their three-hour battle with ETS on Saturday morning, we let them go back to being their old creative selves.

EXTRACURRICULAR ACTIVITIES

Colleges want students who are capable of doing college-level work. They also want students who are interesting. To a large extent, a college's opinion of how interesting you are will be determined by what you do when you're not in class. Your extracurricular activities can play a big part in distinguishing you from other applicants and determining your chances for admission.

Here are some guidelines regarding extracurricular activities:

1. Quantity is less important than quality and commitment.

Some students think that the way to impress an admissions officer is to sign up for every activity their school offers. This is not a good idea. Colleges are not impressed by students with one of everything on their applications—one year of glee club, one year of yearbook, one year of soccer. You're much better off if you're deeply involved in a just a few activities that you remain committed to year after year. Colleges want to see students who rise to leadership positions in interesting activities. They want to see a student who is a sports reporter for the school newspaper as a freshman, assistant sports editor as a sophomore, managing editor as a junior, and editor in chief as a senior. The way to impress an admissions officer is to demonstrate that you can stick with something long enough to become a big deal. You want to demonstrate that you can be a leader.

This doesn't mean you can't become involved in lots of different activities. To the extent that it's possible, you should try to focus your energies enough to enable you to stand out. Just as it is better to take three years of French than to take one year each of French, Spanish, and German, it is better to spend three years rising to a position of importance on the Student Council than it is to join every organization that comes to mind.

2. You don't have to mention all your activities on your application.

Don't try to squeeze in every single activity you've ever been involved in—from a bake sale in ninth grade to the cleanup committee for the junior prom—in the belief that this will impress an admissions officer. Don't pad your list of activities. Concentrate on the ones that were most important to you (and that you were most important in) and don't be afraid to leave out ones that were trivial.

To give you an idea of what we mean, take a look at the following two lists. The first list is an actual listing of activities by one of our students. The second list is *our* version of the same list. Notice that our version is shorter and in a different order. (Following the lists are some specific comments):

First Version
A.F.S. 10
6th Grade Teacher's Assistant 11
Student Senate 10, 11, 12; Secretary 11, President 12
Yearbook 9
Wrestling 9
Delta Club 10, 11, 12
Anrig Award 12
Newspaper 10, 11, 12; Associate Editor 12
Tennis 9, 10, 11, 12; Co-captain 12
Lettermen's Club 10, 11, 12

Revised Version

Student Senate 10, 11, 12; Secretary 11, President 12

Newspaper 10, 11, 12; Associate Editor 12

Delta Club (community service) 10, 11, 12; Hospital Fund
  organizer 12

Tennis 9, 10, 11, 12; Co-captain 12, State Runner-up Doubles
  12

Anrig Award (scholarship and school spirit) 12

As you can see from either list, this kid is no slouch. But
notice how much more impact the revised list has. In the first
list, the student simply listed his activities as he remembered
them. There was no logic to the order. In our revision, we
pruned out the skimpier-sounding activities and strengthened
the important ones. A.F.S., Sixth-Grade Teacher's Assistant,
Yearbook, and Wrestling got too little of the student's time and
attention to deserve mentioning. Including halfhearted activities like this in a list actually weakens it, because they distract
attention from the truly important and impressive activities.
They also raise questions ("Why did he stop teaching?"). The
Delta Club and the Anrig Award both needed explaining: An
admissions officer isn't going to know what they are. We added
an important accomplishment to the Tennis listing. We left off
the Lettermen's Club simply because it seemed unnecessary
after the Tennis listing (obviously this kid earned his varsity
letter). If he had been an officer of the Lettermen's Club, we
would have left it in and mentioned that, but he wasn't.

Of course, ours isn't the only way. How you write your list
will depend on, among other things, how much space you are
given in which to write it. And there aren't many students who
have this sort of material to work with. But the general principle always applies. Trying to fatten up a list of activities often
just makes it look thin.

3. All extracurricular activities are not equally impressive.

As we implied in the previous section, some activities are
more important than others. Here are some of the more impressive activities:

- Student newspaper, especially in leadership positions.
- Student government, especially if you hold an executive office.
- Choir or orchestra, especially if you are a soloist or an officer.
- Varsity sports, particularly if you are a captain or an all-star of some kind.
- Leadership positions with substantial time commitment in organizations or community service activities.
- Activities with a special significance at your school or in your community. If the Harvest Queen is the most important person at your school—more important than the president of the Student Council—and you are the Harvest Queen, don't forget to mention it and explain.
- Anything unusual that took a lot of time and effort, such as being mayor of your town or a volunteer firefighter.
- Eagle Scouts.
- All-state anything.
- Math club (if you're a girl)

Here are some activities you probably shouldn't mention in your application. (We're not saying don't do them; just don't talk about them in your application.)

- Science Fiction Club or any activity having to do with science fiction, including strange computer clubs.
- Anything that would cause you to mention the words "Dungeons and Dragons" in your application.
- Game clubs, especially role-playing game clubs.
- Any radical political organization, especially any radical right-wing political organization. You might not even want to mention the Young Republicans.
- Any fundamentalist religious group.
- Any paramilitary or vigilante organization.

4. Remember why colleges are interested in extracurricular activities.

Colleges are most interested in students who do interesting things, stick with them, and rise to positions of leadership in them. Beyond this, they are most interested in activities that show you have the respect of your peers. You should be careful about putting too much emphasis on activities that don't bring you into contact with other people: reading, hiking, writing poetry. These are great activities and they're worth pursuing, but if they're important to you you want to be sure you're also doing things that demonstrate your ability to be a leader and get along with groups of people.

Science fiction fantasy does not go over big on college applications. If you are addicted to Dungeons and Dragons, keep it to yourself. If you don't, admissions officers will worry that you'll become so involved in your fantasy life that you'll get into trouble with your schoolwork.

Colleges also look for your involvement in activities that reinforce academic or other goals that you mention in your application. If you say in your application that writing is very important to you, you should emphasize activities that gave you opportunities to write.

5. Extracurricular activities can make up for less than stellar grades, but only somewhat.

Students who are deeply involved in extracurricular activities often find that their grades suffer as a result. Admissions officers understand this, but don't believe for a minute that your list of activities will completely make up for mediocre grades. If you want to attend one of the top colleges, remember that there are a lot of high school students out there who are editors of their newspapers *and* straight-A students. Don't overextend yourself to the point where your grades truly suffer.

6. After-school jobs can be impressive, significant activities.

If you can't take part in extracurricular activities because you have to work after school, you won't necessarily be at a disadvantage. Work can be an impressive activity, and you should think about your job in the same way we've told you to think about your activities. You can use your job to convey what a good college candidate you are.

As with other extracurricular activities, the best after-school jobs are the ones you stick with for an extended period and ones in which you rise to positions of responsibility. Simply selling hamburgers at McDonald's is nothing special, but advancing to become a store manager is.

Unusual or creative jobs are better than ordinary after-school, minimum-wage drudgery. If you have the choice (and not everyone does), try to choose a job that makes you seem interesting. If you have to work so that your family can make ends meet, be sure the colleges you apply to know that. Helping to support a family is a serious, adult responsibility, and it demonstrates something good about your character.

If the money you earn after school goes for luxuries like expensive clothes and a fancy stereo, you need to be a little careful about your after-school job. Some students become so wrapped up in earning money that they lose all interest in activities offered by or associated with their schools. A student who helps his family make ends meet looks like a good prospect to an admissions officer; a student who misses out on school government because he's working to meet payments on a Corvette does not.

HOW I SPENT MY SUMMER VACATION

Most of what we've been saying about extracurricular activities and after-school jobs also applies to how you spend your summer vacations. If you have the luxury of choosing how you spend your summers, choose jobs and other activities that help make you the committed, interesting paragon that we've been describing.

QUESTIONS AND ANSWERS

Should I go to summer school at Exeter or Harvard?

Many prep schools and colleges earn money during the summer by conducting classes for high school students and others. Many students have the idea that enrolling in these summer sessions is a ticket to admission at very selective colleges. This is not the case.

First of all, summer sessions at these schools tend to be nowhere near as rigorous as their regular sessions. Surviving Harvard summer school won't make Harvard think you're capable of doing Harvard work.

Second, unless you have a pressing reason for attending one of these summer sessions, you would probably help your chances more by getting an interesting job. Don't sign up for summer school just because you think it will impress the admissions office at Princeton. It won't.

Should I take courses at a local college during the school year?

If your high school really can't satisfy your academic needs (because it doesn't offer calculus or because you've taken all the science courses it offers), you shouldn't hesitate to turn to a local college. Some high schools even have formal arrangements with colleges in their areas. What you should never do, though, is go to a local college to take a course that your high school offers. If you simply look like you're trying to impress an admissions officer, an admissions officer probably won't be impressed.

If you do sign up for college courses, be careful that you don't accumulate too many college credits to be admitted as a freshman at the college you want to attend after high school. Some colleges and universities have restrictions on how many college credits their applicants can earn before matriculation.

Should I drop an extracurricular activity I love just because you say it isn't as impressive to admissions officers as some other activities?

No. You shouldn't become so calculating that you end up doing a lot of things you don't like. The greater danger, though, is that you'll sign up for some boring activity you hate (like trigonometry club) because you think it will impress an admissions officer, when in all likelihood it will end up having the opposite effect.

I got an F in math in ninth grade. Am I screwed?

No and yes. Admissions officers are pretty good about discounting isolated failures, as long as they happen early. If you blow off your entire ninth grade year but then pull yourself together for the rest of high school, most admissions officers won't be unduly bothered.

However, you'll still be left with a grade point average and class rank that are lower than they might have been. When admissions officers flip through your file, they'll notice those numbers and very possibly forget all the ins and outs of your transcript.

I'm listed in *Who's Who Among American High School Students*. Should I mention this in my application?

No. Being listed in the high school *Who's Who* is like being invited to join the National Geographic Society. It doesn't mean anything. Don't try to beef up your application with phony accomplishments. If admissions officers cared about *Who's Who Among American High School Students,* they'd order copies of it. They don't.

CHAPTER 4

YOUR
APPLICATIONS

"The dog ate my application. It really did. Just chewed it up a little, actually. I had about two weeks until the deadline. I had to call the school to get another. Next time, I photocopy everything."

Most students hate filling out applications. They hate answering the questions and they hate having to fill in everything neatly. This is good news for you, because it means that you can improve your chances substantially simply by paying more attention to these details than everybody else does.

In this chapter we'll cover all the basics and alert you to some of the peculiarities you may encounter. Essay questions, faculty recommendations, and interviews will be covered separately in Chapter Five.

WHEN TO DO WHAT

As we told you in Chapter One, you should write away for applications and other information no later than the summer after your junior year and no sooner than the last semester of your junior year. Although we don't think there are many reasons for applying to more than six schools, there's no reason not to send away for lots and lots of applications. Sometimes you can tell from an application itself that a school just isn't the place for you. One of our students was surprised to find that one of the schools he thought he wanted to attend required its applicants to fill out their applications in their own handwriting. "That just seemed stupid," he told us. "I put it off and put it off. Finally, I decided not to apply. Besides, I have terrible handwriting."

When your applications begin to arrive, put them in a safe place where they won't get crumpled. A school's application may be bound inside a publication. (Harvard had a particularly nasty one last year which we completely mangled in doing the research for this book.) Remove it carefully and put it with your other applications. Some guidance counselors advise starting a file for each college. We don't know more than about three people who are organized enough to do this, but if you are, go ahead. The main thing, though, is to keep the application forms from getting beaten up.

When you have accumulated a few applications, get good, clean, clear photocopies made of them. You should probably make *several* copies of each one. (It's worth paying more for good copies; don't use one of those machines at the post office that make smelly gray copies.) Then carefully put the originals and the copies back in a safe place.

When it comes time to fill out applications, always do a rough draft on one of your copies. Making a rough draft will let you see how everything fits. When everything is just right, you can fill out the original. If you screw up the original at this point, don't panic: you have copies. Fill out one of the copies as though it were the original and send it in. Before you send it in, make a copy of the completed version. This copy will be a lifesaver if your original somehow gets mislaid, and it will be a helpful source of information when you are filling out other applications.

If you totally screw up, write a postcard requesting a new application. Don't submit a crummy-looking application simply to avoid the embarrassment of having to ask for a new one. Your request for a new application will be read by a secretary; your crummy-looking application will be read by everyone and will be held against you. If it's really the last minute, you can telephone the admissions office to ask for a new one, but you should never call an admissions office unless it's absolutely, positively necessary.

ROLLING ADMISSION, EARLY DECISION, EARLY ACTION, ETC.

Many colleges offer variations on the standard, single-deadline admission procedure. Here are the most important of these variations, with our comments:

ROLLING ADMISSION
Some schools, primarily big state universities, don't admit their freshmen all at once: They admit them as they go along. If you apply in October, your application is considered in October. If you apply in November, your application is considered in November. Admissions officers keep accepting (and rejecting) students until they have filled the freshman class.

If you are applying to a school that uses rolling admission, it is obviously in your best interest to apply as early as possible. The longer you wait, the more likely you will be to be rejected simply for lack of space.

EARLY DECISION

Some colleges conduct a special admission period before their regular admission period. If you know absolutely that you want to attend a certain college, you may be able to apply early and be notified of your acceptance, deferral, or rejection before your classmates have even begun to fill out their applications. Deadlines for early-decision programs usually fall in November; notifications are usually made in December.

Colleges expect something in return for giving you the chance to do this. One thing they usually expect is a binding commitment from you to attend their college if you are accepted. Some colleges don't even permit early-decision candidates to apply to other schools until after the notification date. Other colleges permit you to apply to other schools but require you to withdraw those applications if you are accepted early decision. Every school's rules are a little different, so be sure you understand the requirements and, especially, the obligations.

In most early-decision programs, few applicants are rejected outright. Usually students who are not admitted are "deferred" into the regular applicant pool, where they are considered again. Because of this, many guidance counselors advise their students to apply early decision (or early action—see below), on the theory that it gives them two chances to be admitted: once in the early pool, and once again in the regular pool.

If you can get it together in time to apply early decision, you could be way ahead. Colleges love to be loved, and you'll have a leg up on the admissions process.

EARLY ACTION

Four Ivy League colleges—Brown, Harvard, Princeton, and Yale—offer a variation on early decision called early action. Applications are due November 1 and notification is made in mid-December, but accepted students don't have to decide what to do until the regular May 1 reply date.

Stay away from early action unless you're confident you'll be accepted. Why? Because applying early action doesn't really give you two chances to be admitted. The early-action pools at these colleges contain disproportionate numbers of very strong candidates. If your credentials aren't as good as theirs, your chances of being accepted will be lower than they would have been in the regular pool, because your application will look worse by comparison.

But won't you be deferred into the regular pool if you don't get in at first?

Yes, but you'll be at a disadvantage. The admissions committee will remember you from the early-action pool, and they will remember you as a person they decided not to admit. They will also remember flaws and weaknesses in your application that they might never have discovered had they not encountered it in the early-decision period, when the competition was tougher.

EARLY IS BETTER THAN LATE

No matter how you apply, it's always better to get your application in early than to wait till the last minute. Admissions officers generally *like* to admit students and feel sad about rejecting them. The earlier in the decision process your application is considered, the less likely it will be to be thrown irretrievably into the Reject pile. Early in the process, admissions officers tend to be more forgiving of borderline applications than they are later on. It's toward the end of the admission period, when deadlines are approaching, that admissions officers begin to get ruthless.

If you somehow miss the application deadline by a few days or even weeks, send your application in anyway and see what happens. Simply sending it in is probably better than calling first. An admissions officer will find it easier to say no to you on the phone than to throw a completed application into the trash.

Remember that you will never get your application in early unless you start working on it promptly. Don't put it off. Many colleges will ask you to fill out a data card or preliminary application before you fill out a full application, or even before they send you one. Do this right away. These forms often ask for basic information that can be computerized, and the colleges need time to get it all entered into their databases.

GENERAL GUIDELINES FOR FILLING OUT APPLICATIONS

No two schools' application forms are exactly alike, although there are lots of similarities. Here are some tips and comments that will help you wade through your pile.

TYPING

As we mentioned earlier, there are a few colleges out there that *require* students to fill out their applications by hand. They think they'll learn something about you by looking at your handwriting. If you are applying to one of those colleges, you should do as you are told. (Never use pencil, by the way. And don't use water-soluble ink—spilled coffee will make it run. Use only blue or black ink. Neat ballpoint or a good erasable pen is best, but don't leave splotches and don't press too hard. If, as is likely, you are applying somewhere else, you *must* type your application (or get someone else to do it for you), and the typing must be neat.

Someone did an experiment a few years ago. Teachers were asked to read a group of student papers. Some of the papers had been typed, and some had been handwritten. What happened? Papers that had been typed were given better grades than *identical* papers that had been handwritten. In school, good typing could make the difference between a B and an A. In applying to college, good typing could make the difference between being admitted and being rejected.

Some other typing tips:
- Use a new, black ribbon.
- Never use a typewriter with a cursive typeface or any other unusual typeface.
- If you have to add extra pages to your application, never

use erasable paper. It looks terrible, it tends to roll up at the edges, and ink smears on it. Use good, heavy bond instead.

▪ If you have to make a lot of corrections on your application, make a photocopy of your finished application and submit the photocopy. This will keep dried correction fluid or chalk from flaking off later on. It will also mask most of the corrections.

▪ Take the time to align your application properly in the typewriter, and be careful to keep your typing within the proper spaces on the page. If your application is in the form of a booklet, carefully take it apart before you try to roll it into the typewriter. Most booklet-type applications have perforated pages so that you can do this.

▪ If you have your applications typed professionally, don't have them typed *so* professionally that it's obvious you didn't do your own typing. In other words, don't have your essays printed by a print shop. You also shouldn't use proportional spacing or justified right-hand margins. You want your application to look neat, not nerdy. And you don't want to make it appear as though your application was not only typed but also written by someone else.

▪ If you're used to using a word processor, be careful. It may help on your essay, but don't even try doing the rest of your application with it. And no dot matrix.

We did hear about one student who used his Apple Macintosh to create a little "newspaper" about himself, complete with professional-looking headlines and articles about his courses, activities, and sports. The newspaper made a big hit with the colleges where it was submitted (the student was accepted everywhere he applied). But this little gimmick was extraordinarily well done. What was impressive was not that it was typeset but that the copy was well written and the whole idea was carried off with humor and skill.

A CONSISTENT STYLE

Newspapers and magazines all have style sheets or style books that enable their writers to remain consistent. They don't want to say "61st Street" today, "sixty-first street" tomorrow, and "61

St." the next day. The style sheet spells out the rules. (We're not talking about writing style here, just consistency.)

You should have a consistent style, too. Consistency matters more than which particular style you choose. If you give your state's name as NY on the first line, don't give it as New York on the fifth.

SPELLING

Misspellings in your application can make you look like a moron. You couldn't do much worse than one girl we know about, who misspelled a college's name three or four times in her application. She was rejected. Students whose applications are messy, ungrammatical, and filled with misspellings look like students who don't care. Your spelling can make a huge difference in your chances—it can make all the difference, especially if you misspell the same common word over and over again. Look up words if you aren't sure how to spell them. And be absolutely certain that you have a good speller proofread everything before you mail it in.

PHOTOGRAPHS

Many colleges ask you to attach a photograph to your application. Usually the photograph is optional. What kind of picture should you attach? Should you attach one at all?

Admissions officers say that seeing photographs of applicants helps them think of applicants as people rather than as pieces of paper. This can work for you or against you. There are circumstances in which you might be better off being considered as a piece of paper. For example, you probably should *not* attach a photograph to your application if you are very overweight. We once saw an application to a selective college on which an admissions officer had scrawled the note "Too fat?"

Female applicants probably should not use photographs that make them look too glamorous, beautiful, or sexy. There are a lot of men out there who think that beautiful women are dumb; there are a lot of women who are jealous of beautiful women.

You should not attach a photograph in which you are poorly

or messily dressed, or in which your hair is uncombed, or in which you look drugged or asleep. If you use a photograph, you should use one that makes you look bright, lively, and healthy. Don't use a funny picture or one that's too "artistic." Don't use a photograph that shows you smoking a cigarette, holding a can of beer, or sitting in the front seat of your Porsche. You also shouldn't use a photograph that looks as though it is calculated to impress admissions officers—such as a picture of you being given an award. (Although we do know a student from the Midwest who made a big hit with admissions officers at one school by using a picture of himself standing beside his prize-winning heifer.) Because formal yearbook photos all look pretty much alike, you might consider *not* using yours. A clear, focused, head-and-shoulders color snapshot might be better.

INTENDED MAJOR

Some colleges and universities offer special programs—such as nursing or engineering—with separate admissions. If you're interested in one of these, you may have to declare your intentions on your application, or even fill out a special application. Read the fine print.

Many other colleges will ask you to state your probable major, if you know it. Be careful how you answer. Your response can affect your chances of being admitted. Here are some things to keep in mind:

▪ Be absolutely certain that your "intended" major is a major offered by the college. If you say you're going to be a journalism major, you'd better be certain the college *has* journalism majors. Remember that offering a course in a field is not the same thing as offering a major in it. If you declare your interest in a field that doesn't exist at that school, the admissions officers will think you are not serious.

▪ You should avoid mentioning the Joe Bloggs majors—premed, pre-law, and, to a lesser extent, business administration—if you can help it. (Some schools have special pre-med and pre-law programs that you have to sign up for ahead of time, but most schools don't.) At the moment colleges are being overrun by eager preprofessionals who love to talk about how much money they're going to make after they graduate. Admissions officers are sick to death of reading applications written by these people. The less you sound like them, the better off you'll be. (If you finally insist on being pre-med or pre-law, be absolutely certain the college offers a major with that name before you write it on your application. Most colleges don't have "premed" or "pre-law" majors.)

▪ Don't claim that you want to be a math major (or an engineering major) if your math SAT scores are mediocre. Don't claim you want to be a biology major if your high school science grades were low. Colleges will hold it against you if your credentials don't back you up. They'll think you don't know what you're talking about.

▪ College administrators and professors have been complaining lately that students don't major in the humanities (literature, languages, art history, etc.) any more. Saying you want to major in one of these, assuming you do, might be a good way to distinguish yourself from Joe Bloggs. Another good way to distinguish yourself is to major in, say, biology with no intention of going on to medical school. If you want to be a bio major but don't want to be a doctor, find a way to say so in your application.

▪ "Undecided" is a perfectly acceptable major if the college doesn't require you to declare something specific. In fact, "undecided" would be a good response for anyone who secretly wants to be pre-med or pre-law. You won't be lying when you say you haven't decided, because it could all be decided for you by your grade in organic chemistry.

INTENDED CAREER

Undecided is the safest answer. Medicine and law are the worst. (This is sometimes just a trick question to find out if you're a pre-med.) Teaching is probably the best at the moment. But no one says seventeen- and eighteen-year-olds have to know what they're going to do with their lives. Some admissions officers *prefer* applicants who haven't made up their minds.

Almost as bad as saying you want to be a doctor or a lawyer is saying you want to "help people" or "work with people." These are Joe Bloggs answers, too, and admissions officers hear them constantly. (Besides, almost any job will permit you to "work with people.")

INTENDED LIVING ARRANGEMENTS

At some colleges, dormitory space places a limit on the number of students who can be accepted, and applicants who plan to live off-campus sometimes have an increased chance of being admitted. This is not always true. Do your homework.

ACTIVITIES, AWARDS, EMPLOYMENT

Unless you're specifically told to do something else, the order in which you list these should reflect some combination of their importance to you and their probable importance in the eyes of admissions officers. Concentrate on the areas in which you've made the longest commitment and achieved the most responsibility. (Reread Chapter Three for more advice on how to present your activities.) Don't feel you have to mention *everything*. If you list a lot of trivial activities you'll appear as though you're trying to put one over on the admissions committee.

In listing jobs, you should make your jobs sound interesting if possible, but you shouldn't make it appear as though you've been reading one of those books on how to write a resumé. If you spent the summer working as a housekeeper, say you were a housekeeper; don't say you were a "domestic engineer." If there was something truly unusual about what you did, be sure you get it in, but don't exaggerate. If you were editor in chief of your school newspaper, be sure to mention that, but don't add that you were "responsible for assigning, receiving, editing, typesetting, laying out, and pasting up articles on a wide variety of topics." That's what editors in chief are supposed to do. If you spell it all out you'll sound like a huckster.

You should, however, go into specifics if the activity is unfamiliar or if you did something noteworthy that isn't mentioned anywhere else in your application. You should also mention specifics if the specifics aren't clearly implied in the name of the activity or your title. If you directed three student plays, don't just write down "Drama"—spell out what you did. But be straightforward about it.

TRAVEL

Many applications will ask you to list recent travel experiences. Admissions officers like students who've seen a bit of the country or the world. You want to be careful, though, not to sound like a little rich brat. Play down the glitzy side of your trips, if there was one. If you paid for all or part of your trip yourself, mention how you earned the money. Most interesting are trips that show creativity, initiative, and independence on your part —like the summer you spent leading an expedition across Nepal with the money you earned working for the Jet Propulsion Laboratory. Much less interesting is the clothes-buying jaunt to Paris you took with your stepmother.

ALUMNI RELATIVES

Most colleges will ask you if you have relatives who attended the same school. Children of alumni and other "legacies" have an admissions advantage everywhere. Don't leave anybody out.

OTHER APPLICATIONS

You may very well be asked to list the other colleges to which you are applying. Admissions officers ask this question for several reasons. The most important one is probably that your answer to it will give them some idea of how serious you are about attending their school. If College X asks you where you are applying, and College X is the most selective school on your list, College X will know that you probably aren't counting on being admitted to College X and that your realistic first choice is someplace else. Everything else being equal, an applicant for whom a particular school is a clear first choice will have an advantage over an applicant for whom it is not.

How does a college know that it's your first choice? There are many ways, some direct and some indirect. An admissions officer may come right out and ask you in an interview. More important, though, are clues scattered throughout your application. If you are really enthusiastic about a school, your enthusiasm will show through. The depth of your familiarity with a college is also a good indication of the strength of your desire to go there. There's nothing wrong with letting each school know how much you value its particular strengths; make them all feel wanted. After all, you won't really know which is your first choice until you've learned where you've gotten in.

Your list of other colleges—even the order in which you write it—will also give admissions officers a little peek into the way your mind works and how you evaluate your own abilities. If the schools you list are all less selective than your credentials suggest you could get into, admissions officers may decide you don't think much of your academic abilities. You should also look at your list again and see if there's a common theme.

How you answer this question isn't that big a deal. But you can never tell what will stick in the mind of an admissions officer, and you should not be hasty in filling in your answers. Don't lie. But if you're applying to a lot of dissimilar schools, your answer doesn't have to be exhaustive. No matter what, don't list more than four or five other schools. If you're applying very early in the application period, you can simply list one or two other schools and say you're undecided about others. Keep in mind that other forms in your file, such as your FAF, may also list the colleges to which you're applying. The most important piece of advice we can give you also applies to every other question on every other application you fill out: Before you answer any question you should ask yourself, "What does my answer say about me?"

RACIAL BACKGROUND

Most applications will give you the option of describing your race or ethnic background. Go ahead and check one of the boxes. Don't check "Other" and then fill in some complicated description of yourself, even if it's accurate. For more on race, and situations in which you should *not* check a box, see Chapter Six.

QUESTIONS AND ANSWERS

Should I lie?

Good question, Almost everybody asks it.

Admissions officers say they can always tell when applicants are lying. That's a lie. But lying is a bad idea anyway. For one thing, it's hard to do. Liars have to have very good memories. They have to be able to tell the story the same way every time, which is a lot easier if the story is true.

It is possible and necessary to tell the truth without telling the *whole* truth. There is nothing wrong with being selective in what you talk about in your application. And there's nothing wrong with not answering questions that haven't been asked. If the application doesn't ask you if you were ever suspended, don't feel you have to confess that you were. If being editor of the literary magazine was a joke at your school, keep it to yourself.

Should I take advantage of "common applications"?

Some colleges have tried to simplify the lives of their applicants by agreeing on a single application form and permitting students to apply to more than one school by using it. This is a nice idea in theory, but you should avoid it like the plague.

The common application always works against you. No school will feel like your first choice if all it knows about you is contained in a photocopy of your application to somewhere else. You can't really tailor a common application to the particular strengths or features of particular schools. It's hard enough to stand out as it is; it will be impossible if you adopt an assembly-line approach.

What if there isn't enough room to fit everything in?

You can get a very good idea of how much a college wants to hear about you by looking at how much room they've left for you to say it in. Generally speaking, they don't want you to add a lot of extra sheets to your application. If they give you tiny spaces in which to list your activities, don't attach a resumé.

This is where a rough draft becomes especially important.

Figure out how much space your answers will take up before you begin typing your final application. Don't squeeze lines together and don't type sideways in the margins. If you have to, abbreviate, but do it in a clear, consistent way. Nonetheless, it's better to add pages than squeeze into the margins.

What if I win the Nobel Prize after I send in my application?

Write a letter letting the admissions office know. The letter will be placed in your folder.

Should I ever, ever, ever draw a little smiley face anywhere on my application?

No. And don't dot your i's with little circles, either.

CHAPTER 5

Essays, Recommendations, and Interviews

"When I was a junior, I helped
out in the admissions office by
giving first readings to applications. The dean of admissions
had a notebook in which everybody would copy out the dumbest
things from people's applications. We spent a lot of time
laughing. And the notebook was
very fat."

For many students, writing application essays, securing good recommendations, and coming across well in interviews are the most unbearable parts of applying to college. They certainly require care and planning. But they don't have to make you depressed.

While your SAT scores and your grades will be the most conspicuous elements of your application folder, the real debate about whether to admit you or reject you may very well concern how you come across in your essays, recommendations, and interviews. If you handle them well, you can substantially increase your chances for admission.

WRITING ESSAYS: FUNDAMENTALS

Virtually all selective colleges will ask you to write at least one essay as part of your application. Admissions officers think of your essay as a little window into your personality. They also see it as evidence of how well you write, which is something they care about a great deal. Colleges are very worried that their students don't write as well as students did in the past. An applicant with strong writing skills has a very big edge.

An admissions officer explained it to us this way: "You just know that a kid who writes well is going to do well in college courses. When faculty members talk to us about admissions, writing comes up frequently. They say, 'When are you going to start admitting students who can write complete sentences?' Good writers make the professors happy, and happy professors make us happy. It's also usually true that a student who writes well enough to be noticed by an admissions officer will also have put together a solid record in high school. It's easy to admit a kid like that."

No guidebook can teach you how to write. Good writers don't become good writers by memorizing a few rules. But we can give you some guidelines that should help you avoid some major pitfalls:

1. Don't use six-dollar words.

One of the worst things young writers do is "beef up" their compositions by substituting long, difficult words for short, easy ones. Some students write a rough draft in their own words and then use a thesaurus to plug in big, impressive words.

Doing this is always obvious, and it is never impressive. A good writer can spot a "thesaurusized" composition a mile away. The reason is that the big, plugged-in words seldom mean exactly what the young writer thinks they do. There are few precise synonyms in English. Most of the big words in a thesaurus have meanings that are different from the meanings of the shorter words they replace.

2. Good writing is writing that is easily understood.

You want to get your point across, not bury it in words. Flowery writing is not good writing. Your prose should be clear and direct. You will be in trouble if an admissions officer has to struggle to figure out what you are trying to say.

3. Avoid adjectives and adverbs.

As you reread your essays, stop at every adjective or adverb and ask yourself if it is necessary. Too many adjectives and adverbs make writing seem flabby. Concentrate on nouns and verbs.

4. Avoid the word *however*.

Most people use it incorrectly or put it in places where it isn't needed. Few people know how to put punctuation around it. Everyone uses it too much.

5. Buy and read *The Elements of Style*, by William Strunk, Jr., and E. B. White.

This little book is a required investment for any writer. You'll use it again and again and again in college and beyond. If you do what it says, your writing will improve. Get a copy tomorrow and read it twice.

6. Don't use exclamation points.

Ever!

7. Throw away your copy of *Bartlett's Familiar Quotations*.

One of the worst things a student essay can contain is a lot of sentences that begin, "As Shakespeare said . . ." or, "I am reminded of Tennyson's words. . . ." Admissions officers will know you found these lines in a book of quotations. They won't think you pulled them out of your memory. Quotations make essays seem phony, not sophisticated.

Don't begin your essay with a little quotation, either—no matter how perfect it seems. And don't *ever* quote the lyrics of a rock song.

8. Don't put quotation marks around words that aren't quotations.

Don't put quotation marks around a word just because it isn't quite the "right" word for what you want to say. If the word doesn't seem "right" without quotation marks around it, find one that does.

9. Don't say what you're going to say, say that you're going to say it, say it, say it again, and say that you've said it. Instead, simply say it.

Most student compositions have tedious introductions and conclusions that first announce and then repeat whatever is said between them. Most good writers don't write this way. Even if they did, you wouldn't have room to do it on your application. You want to make sure a reader understands what you're talking about, but you also want to be concise. You don't want to bore an already bored admissions officer with a boring introductory paragraph that does little more than repeat the question.

10. Have a good writer critique your essay. Have a good speller proofread it.

Admissions officers take it for granted that applicants get help with their essays. In fact, if you submit an essay that is filled with misspellings and grammatical errors, admissions officers will conclude not only that you don't know how to write but also that you aren't shrewd enough to get help. Ask your mom, dad, teacher, brother, sister, *someone* to read your essay and comment on it. (Does it sound phony? Is it clear? Do I get my point across? Is it boring? Are the jokes stupid?) Be especially careful about punctuation. *Most high school students don't know where to put commas.* Find someone who knows. You should also critique your own essay after letting it sit for at least a few days. The longer it sits, the more mistakes you'll be able to find.

Asking for help isn't cheating (although actually getting someone else to *write* your essay is.)

11. Put a lid on it.

Unless they specifically tell you otherwise, admissions officers would prefer that you confine your responses to the spaces provided for them. Longer is not better. Don't add extra pages because you think length is impressive. It isn't. Your essay will be the zillionth essay exactly like it that most of its readers have read. Do them a favor and be brief.

WRITING ESSAYS: TOPICS, ATTITUDES, APPROACHES

Your newly honed writing skills won't do you much good if you don't have anything interesting to write about. Most of your essay topics will be assigned, but some will probably be left up to you. Even if they are assigned, you will have a great deal of leeway in terms of approach. Here are some guidelines that should help you zero in on a good topic or, if the topic is assigned, help you find an effective way to get your points across.

1. Don't repeat information from other parts of your application.

An application doesn't give you much room to make your case. Don't waste space (and bore your readers) by repeating yourself.

For example, an application may ask you on one page to list your extracurricular activities and on another to write a brief essay describing what your activities mean to you. *Don't use the essay simply to repeat the list in expanded form.* You would be shocked at the number of students who do this. Admissions officers *hate* it.

Instead of repeating yourself, take advantage of the opportunity to expand on information you've already provided. Write about something interesting that you did or that happened to you in one of your activities. If your list of activities includes something really outstanding that won't be immediately obvious to an admissions officer, use this essay to make sure it comes across.

2. In general, avoid generalities.

Admissions officers have to read an unbelievable number of essays, most of which are boring. You will find it harder to be boring if you write about particulars. If you are called upon to write about your extracurricular activities, don't write an essay about activities in general: "Extracurricular activities are important to me because they enable me to expand my horizons," etc. Instead, *narrow* your focus. Write about something particular that happened to you in a particular activity. It's the details that stick in a reader's mind. If you're writing about your trip to Europe, don't give your itinerary. Focus in on an interesting detail: a fascinating old man, the time you got lost in Florence, the day you helped a Parisian fix his car.

This rule even applies to questions that seem to *demand* general answers. For example, many colleges ask students to write a few paragraphs about why they want to attend that particular college. One popular answer has to do with the value of "obtaining a good liberal arts education," or something similar. This answer is about as interesting as a sleeping pill, and you probably don't mean it anyway. You may not be able to give a really truthful answer ("Because I want to ski all the time"), but you can at least try to give an interesting one. You might talk about a particular course you want to take, or about a specific gap in your knowledge that you want to fill. The less general and vague your answer is—and the more you actually mean it —the more likely it is to be interesting.

One good way to avoid generalities is to write about people. Instead of writing about "a good liberal arts education," write about a person you admire who went to the same college. Instead of writing about how well your high school education prepared you for college, write about a teacher who made a big impression on you. The more specific you are, the more readable your essay will be.

Sometimes an application will try to nudge you in this direction by giving you a fairly specific question to answer ("Describe a teacher who meant a lot to you"). Don't defeat the purpose of this kind of question by hurrying as quickly as possible back into generalities. That is, don't write about a teacher who changed your life by showing you "the value of a good liberal arts education."

3. Be humorous if you can, but be careful.

One good joke can get you into Yale. No kidding. A student who can make an admissions officer laugh never gets lost in the shuffle. The joke is read aloud, everyone smiles, no one can bear to throw you into the reject pile.

But beware. Most people think they're funny, but only a few really are. Most attempts at humor in college applications are counterproductive. Humor can help you, but you must use it carefully and sparingly.

In general, you will be better off if you strive to make your reader smile, not laugh. The closer you stick to your own life and your own experiences, the more successful you will be. Most of us are more successful at recounting humorous incidents from our lives than at making up jokes from scratch.

Most writers ruin jokes by beating readers over the head with them. Don't write, "A funny thing that happened to me the other day was. . . ." or "I really had to laugh when. . . ." If your story is really funny, you don't need to label it. And don't do the equivalent of nudging your reader with your elbow. The most successful joke is often the one told with a straight face.

4. Maintain the proper tone.

Your essay should be informal without being sloppy, witty without being childish, memorable without being outrageous. If read aloud, your essay should sound like good conversation. You want to warm your reader, not overwhelm him or her. You want to be casual without being chatty or cutesy.

5. Don't write about what Joe Bloggs writes about.

An article about college admissions in the Kansas City *Star* a couple of years ago described the essay-reading experience of Parke Muth, assistant dean of admissions at the University of Virginia: "This last academic year, Mr. Muth says, his university received 16,000 applications for 2,600 places, and he read 3,000 essays on participation in a summer program for gifted students and 3,000 on the students' travels around Europe with the theme 'It's a small world, after all.' "

Here are some other topics you should probably avoid. Some of them are simply bad topics that are inappropriate for college applications. Others are extremely popular topics that make admissions officers' eyes glaze over. For one reason or another, don't write about:

▪ Your relationship with your girlfriend or your boyfriend. Important to you, but a little creepy to an admissions officer.

▪ Your religious beliefs. Deeply religious students make admissions officers nervous—*unless you're applying to a college with a strong religious orientation,* in which case an essay about your religious views would probably be in order.

▪ Your conservative political views.

▪ Any other political views. Have you ever had a political discussion with someone who didn't agree with you? Did you end up shouting at each other? People have a tendency to become upset very quickly with people whose political beliefs are different from their own. Avoid politics altogether and you won't run the risk of offending a reader. If you do write about a political experience—say, the summer you spent working on a congressman's reelection campaign—avoid ideology as much as possible and write about the nuts and bolts of running the campaign.

- The evils of drugs. Drugs are indeed evil, but student essays on this subject tend to sound goody-goodyish and contrived.
- The pleasures of drugs. For obvious reasons.
- Sex.
- The first time you got drunk, or any other time you got drunk.
- A classmate who was killed in a car accident. This is a standard topic, seldom handled well. Death is very hard to write about. Student essays about the death of a friend or parent are sometimes extraordinarily moving; more often, though, they sound either contrived or overly emotional. If you decide to write about a topic like this, be sure you're up to it.
- How much you love yourself. Don't write an essay that makes it sound as though you spend a lot of time sitting around thinking about yourself. All adolescents spend a lot of time thinking about themselves. Adults are tired of hearing about it. You'll make a better impression if you write about something that makes you seem like a great person rather than simply coming out and claiming to be great.
- The importance of a college education. There just aren't that many observations you could make that an admissions officer wouldn't have heard a million times before. Joe Bloggs is irresistibly attracted to this topic, because he thinks it will make him seem serious. Instead, it usually makes him seem vacuous.
- Your personal philosophy, particularly if it involves any form of selfishness. Many, many essays are some variation on this theme. Generally speaking, *nobody's* personal philosophy is very interesting to anyone else.
- Your SAT scores. Never, never, never mention your SAT scores, no matter how good or how bad. In fact, never mention them again to anyone.
- How much you like to party, screw around, etc.
- Any topic that doesn't appeal to you but that you think will appeal to an admissions officer, such as how you have recently discovered the importance of studying hard. Essays like this make the Phoniness Alarms go off.

• Anything that will make a reader blush or feel embarrassed.

• Anything that will incidentally reveal you to be a poor college prospect—such as an essay on how much you hate to study.

• Big ideas, such as your plan for how to make the world live together in peace. These almost always flop. Stick to details and particulars.

• Trendy topics, such as apartheid (unless you are a black South African), the threat of nuclear war, or anything involving current events. You probably won't come up with anything new to say. These essays, no matter what the intentions of the writer, tend to be predictable and boring.

• Anything that makes it sound as though the only reason you want to go to college is so you can make a whole lot of money when you get out. Admissions officers don't make much money, and they're sick of greedy teenagers.

• Solitary pursuits. In general, activities that involve interacting with other people make better topics than activities you do alone. You don't want to make admissions officers worry that you won't get along with your classmates. (This is really only a problem if virtually every activity you mention in your application is solitary.)

• How much psychotherapy has changed your life. You don't want admissions officers to worry that there is a danger of your going crazy while in school.

• How glad you are to be National Merit semifinalist or how pleased you were to be named valedictorian of your class. This is like writing about your SAT scores.

• "The Best Game of My Life" or other athletic incidents written in glib style.

• Any topic specifically mentioned as a great essay topic in a popular how-to-get-into-college book. Joe Bloggs reads those books, too.

6. Write about something you really care about.

Even genuinely bad writers can turn out a readable essay if the topic means something to them. The motorcycle you built from scratch, the time you helped deliver a baby in a snowstorm, the day you taught your little brother to tie his shoes. The good topic is the one you *want* to write about, not the one you think you *ought* to write about—while always keeping in mind who your audience is.

The way to approach finding a topic is first to ask yourself what you want to write and then to ask yourself whether an admissions officer will want to read it.

7. Remember what the point of an application essay is.

With your essay you want to prove two things: that you are a decent writer and that you are an interesting, mature person. By contrast, Joe Bloggs thinks that the point of his essay is to prove to the admissions committee that he is serious about education. Admissions officers hear this constantly, and it bores them. "My summer in France taught me the value of a solid background in a foreign language . . ."; "The summer I spent at Andover summer school showed me the value of good study skills . . ."; "I never realized how important a good education was until I . . ." Nobody *really* thinks like this. It almost always sounds contrived in an essay.

Instead of trying to think of things you've done that will make you seem more serious, try to think of things that have made you more interesting.

8. Every story doesn't need a moral.

Many students feel they have to make a direct connection between whatever they write about and their suitability for college. Many essays convey the impression that their authors have never done anything that didn't groom them in some way for higher education. This, too, sounds contrived. If you write a good essay, you won't need to tell admissions officers why you wrote it.

9. Don't apologize, don't explain.

Don't use an essay to explain bad grades, low SAT scores, drug arrests, suspensions, or any other black marks in your record. Explanations usually just make these sound worse. They certainly draw attention to your weaknesses.

If there really is something about your grades that should be explained, your guidance counselor should do it. But don't ask your guidance counselor to write a letter simply explaining that you are smarter than your SAT scores. It may be true, but admissions officers have heard it a million times.

Some applications will allow you to explain peculiarities in your record that you think need explaining. You may do so if you feel you must, but tread carefully here. Explaining a difficulty often does little more than draw attention to it, which makes it seem worse.

If an application asks you right out, as some do, whether you have ever been suspended and why, you'll have to answer truthfully. But unless you have a very, very good reason for doing so, you shouldn't answer this question unless it is asked.

10. Submit extra materials if they're called for.

Some colleges permit you to submit extra materials—poems, musical compositions or tapes, short stories, artwork, and so on. Some colleges don't want you to do this, and say so in their applications. Check.

Anything extra that you submit should genuinely enhance your application. Be realistic about your abilities. Submitting half a dozen unexceptional poems will make the poetry award you won seem less impressive. The same might be true of stories you wrote for a local newspaper. Before you let admissions officers see exactly what you did, be certain it doesn't sound better in the abstract.

Don't try to be too cute with extra submissions. Applicants sometimes endear themselves to admissions committees by sending homemade cookies or other clever creations. But be very careful. Gimmicky extras like this usually backfire.

Whatever you do, make certain your submissions are neat and well presented.

TYPICAL QUESTIONS, TYPICAL ANSWERS

Here's a selection of common types of essay question, followed by some Joe Bloggs responses to them and recommendations for avoiding the Joe Bloggs mentality.

Write about someone you admire.

This question has many forms. Bowdoin's is, "Do you have any heroes? Explain." Joe Bloggs tends to write without much conviction about people like the president of the United States, his father (Joseph Bloggs, Sr.), Mother Teresa, or Martin Luther King, Jr. These may all be highly admirable, heroic people, but they seldom inspire interesting essays. The best responses are ones that are both meaningful to the writer and somewhat surprising to the reader. You don't want to *stun* the reader (by writing about Hitler, for example—never a good idea), but you do want to give him or her something unusual to think about.

Write about something you have read.

A number of colleges will ask you some version of this question. Many applicants are attracted to it because it seems so easy —all you have to do is write a book report. But that's the danger: Too many responses to this sort of question sound like book reports, and nobody likes to read book reports. The advice we gave you about the "someone you admire" question applies to this one as well: Don't write about an obvious book. Your choice should make you seem interesting (though not eccentric).

Most important, if you are asked to write about a book, be certain you write about a book: Don't write about your favorite movie.

Why do you want to attend this school?

Your real reason may be something better left unstated ("Because I want to party and screw around for four years"), but the closer to the truth your answer is the more likely you'll be to write something that an admissions officer will enjoy reading. Avoid Joe Bloggs generalities ("to get a good liberal arts education," "to broaden my knowledge") and think in terms of specifics.

Harvard's version of this question is "Write a brief statement describing your academic goals." Too many students, when faced with this type of question, ignore the word "academic" and write about their *career* goals. They are not the same thing. Again, specifics are better than generalities. Don't write, "Because I believe I have something to contribute to your prestigious . . ."

How do you see yourself ten years from now?

Joe Bloggs sees himself as a lawyer or a doctor. If you do, too, don't say so. In fact, avoid using this question as an opportunity to describe any type of job you think you'd like to have. This is a tough question, because the temptation to be boring can be overpowering. If you avoid employment as a topic, though, you'll be well ahead of the game. Instead, narrow your focus. Picture yourself doing something a bit unusual, and don't strain to make a direct connection between it and a college education. Just as it is a mistake to act as though your entire life has been building towards your freshman year at College X, you don't want to pretend that you think your college degree will be the sole foundation on which you build the rest of your life.

Write about a meaningful activity.

Yale's version of this question is, "Which activity or interest has meant the most to you? Why?" The best place to start looking for an answer is the truth: Which of your activities really *was* the most meaningful to you? Which was the most fun? Which did you look forward to? Don't say that your most meaningful activity was your service on the Student Council because it taught you the importance of effective leadership. "Effective leadership" was *not* why you liked the Student Council, assuming that you did. On this type of question, Joe Bloggs tries too hard to make himself seem serious, motivated, and directed. He really ought to be trying to make himself seem interesting.

RECOMMENDATIONS

Most selective colleges ask their applicants to submit two recommendations from teachers. These can have an important bearing on your chances—particularly if they are negative. Here are some guidelines that should help you secure better recommendations:

1. Be prompt.

Teachers have too much to do as it is. Writing recommendations takes a lot of time, especially if you attend a big school and the teachers you ask are popular. Give your recommenders plenty of time. (The earlier you are, the less likely your recommenders are to be buried in recommendation forms already.)

2. Make it easy for them.

When you ask teachers to write recommendations for you, give them everything they need, including your application deadline and a stamped, addressed envelope. Some guidance counselors and books recommend that you also give your recommenders a list of your activities, to remind them of what you've been up to for the last few years. We don't think this is a good idea. Too many recommenders simply rehash students' accomplishments—information that is already in their applications. If your recommender has your brag list sitting there in front of him, he will be unlikely to do much more than turn it into sentences and paragraphs. Admissions officers will wonder why you picked a recommender who obviously knew so little about you.

3. Waive your rights.

You have the legal right to read the stuff colleges have in their files about you. Virtually all recommendation forms include a little box where you can waive this right by signing your name. By all means, waive the right. Colleges won't pay attention to your recommendations if they think the people who wrote them were worried that you would be reading them. Sign the waiver before you give the forms to your teachers.

4. Pick wisely.

The actual content of a recommendation isn't the only important thing about it. To a large degree, a recommendation is also a test of your judgment. If your recommendations are negative or wishy-washy, admissions officers will conclude that you aren't bright enough to pick good recommenders. In general, when choosing recommenders, you should do the following:

- Pick teachers who know and like you.
- Pick teachers who will absolutely positively write positive things about you. This is important enough to discuss openly with your teachers. If you feel uneasy about asking a teacher directly whether he or she will write you a strong recommendation, you can do the same thing indirectly by giving the teacher an out. You might say something like, "I don't want to put you in a spot if you'd prefer not to do this." If the teacher feels uneasy about recommending you, this gives him or her a way to decline without coming right out and telling you you're a jerk. Another way to do the same thing even more indirectly would be to say something like, "I need a strong recommendation, but I know you're busy. Would you have time to write one for me?"
- Pick teachers in fields where your principal interests lie. If you say in your application that you are going to be an English major, at least one or your recommendations should be from an English teacher.
- Pick teachers who are reliable. This is also a test of your judgment. If a teacher doesn't get your recommendation in on time, *you* will be the one who looks bad.
- Pick teachers who are good writers. Nothing is less impressive than a poorly written recommendation.
- If possible and appropriate, pick a teacher who went to the college you want to attend. This probably won't be possible, but you may be able to choose a teacher who went to a similar school, or one of the same caliber. If you're applying to an Ivy League school, a teacher with an Ivy League degree will be in a good position to certify that you are capable of doing Ivy League work. No matter where they went to school, teachers

who are familiar with the schools to which you are applying are in a better position to write good recommendations.

5. Send a thank-you note.

Thanking a recommender is good manners. It's also a polite way to remind a forgetful teacher to get on the stick. Send your thank-you note a week or two before the deadline. If writing a note makes you feel uncomfortable, you can thank the recommender in person. It will still serve as a reminder. A hint: Thank your recommender when he is sitting at his desk, not when he is running down the hall. Your reminder will be more likely to produce the desired result if pen and paper are at hand.

6. Don't submit (many) extra recommendations.

Fattening your folder with recommendations from every teacher in your school will just make you look pushy. Likewise with recommendations from powerful or famous friends of your parents. We know a student whose father got a U.S. senator to write a recommendation for him. The senator wrote a very flattering letter—about the father. The student was rejected. When the student's guidance counselor asked the college why the student had been rejected, the college said it had been tempted to admit the father, who sounded very interesting, but had decided against it in the end. Letters from famous people almost always seem pushy and show-offy, even if they are informative and sincere.

You *can* submit one or two extra recommendations if they are from people who really do know you well and who really are in a position to say interesting things about you. If you made a big splash at a volunteer job, a letter from your boss could help you. This kind of letter can fill out an admissions officer's image of your personality, revealing the human characteristics that a teacher's recommendations may not.

One of our students was helped considerably by an unsolicited letter from a summer employer. The employer said in his letter that he had given the student a job because he had owed a favor to his father and that he hadn't expected much of him. But the student had worked hard and done magnificently and won the respect of everyone in the office. He said that he would be happy to have the boy in his company full-time and that he could tell he would be a success at whatever he put his hand to. The letter wasn't terribly long, but it was obviously heartfelt and it made a big impression.

INTERVIEWS

Few schools require on-campus interviews. Some don't offer them. Some have elaborate networks of alumni who interview applicants in their areas. Some schools conduct informal interviews with students who need information.

Before you write to an admissions office to arrange "an interview," make sure you understand what kind, if any, the school offers or requires. One of our students told us that the most embarrassing moment of her life was strolling into an admissions office and discovering from a staff member that interviews aren't given.

Most interviews aren't as important as students generally assume. At some colleges, all interviews are handled by the most junior members of the admissions staff. Still, interviews do make impressions. Some students are admitted simply because they had great interviews; less often, students are rejected because they bombed.

Here are a few guidelines:

1. Do your homework.

Don't ask questions that are answered in the brochures you've been sent. This means you have to read those brochures. Ugh! Read them one at a time, at breakfast before each interview.

If there is a popular conception of the school (Princeton is isolated, Dartmouth has too many fraternities, Harvard has too little student-teacher contact), *don't* ask about it. Your interviewer will have heard the same question ten billion times. He or she will also have spent the last few weeks reviewing a seemingly endless procession of Joe Bloggses. You don't want to seem off the wall by asking bizarre questions; but even more you don't want to sound exactly like the boring JB who was in there before you.

Don't ask questions if you have no interest in the answers. Unless you have a real reason for wanting to know how many of a college's graduates go on to graduate school, don't ask. The question will make you sound dopey, not smart and serious. And don't read questions from a list. Students who do this look either scatterbrained or nerdy. If you've spent time on campus, ask questions on the information you've gained.

2. Don't give dumb answers.

Before you go to an interview, you need to have a pretty good idea of how you'll answer several stock questions if they're asked. Some of these questions are: Why do you want to go here? What first brought us to your attention? What do you want to major in? What do you want to do with your life?

Most students have a hard time answering questions like this. The trouble with them is that they force you to think specifically about reasons that you probably haven't examined very carefully. But thinking about them is helpful as well as necessary. If you can put your finger on an intelligent and convincing reason why you want to attend a school, not only your interview but also your application will begin to fall into place. The important thing is to be prepared for the "easy ones" so that you don't have to stammer and clear your throat when the admissions officer asks them.

3. Make it easy for your interviewer.

Conviviality, poise, and aplomb are three qualities that have little to do with how good a student you are but a lot to do with how your interview goes. You want to seem bright, interested, mature, and at ease. The more comfortable your interviewer feels at your interview, the better the impression you'll make. If the conversation lags, ask a question.

4. Unless you're asked specifically—and we mean specifically—don't mention your SAT scores or your grades.

We've said this several times already, but it can't be said enough. One of the most boring and predictable things you can do in an interview is try to sneak in your SAT scores. We even know a student who scored 1400 and said in an interview that he was disappointed in his scores. Obviously he wasn't disappointed. He just wanted to mention those big numbers. The admissions officer thought he was a creep. You will hurt your chances for admission if you make an admissions officer think you are a creep.

A former Ivy League admissions officer once told us about a game she used to play with pushy applicants from certain high schools. She would keep asking questions that she knew would give the students opportunities to work in their SAT scores; then, every time they were about to mention them, she would change the subject. This drove the applicants crazy and kept the admissions officer alert during interviews that she otherwise didn't enjoy. Needless to say, not many of these students received acceptances.

Now, you may say that it's unfair for admissions officers to put so much emphasis on SAT scores and then not want to hear you talk about them. But whoever said life was fair? Don't worry. Your scores are the first thing the admissions officer will look at when he or she picks up your folder. You don't need to wave a flag.

5. Look the part.

Get a respectable haircut. Don't chew gum. Wear nice clothes, but don't look slick (sport coat or skirt, not three-piece suit or party dress). If you're a boy, take out your earring. No matter who you are, clean your fingernails. Brush your teeth. Don't smoke. Wash behind your ears. And in front of them, too. You can go back to being a slob once they let you in.

6. Send your parents to Antarctica.

You definitely shouldn't let your parents try to accompany you to your interview. It's better to keep them out of the building altogether. Parents can only hurt; they never help. We know a brilliant kid who was rejected by a top Ivy League college *solely* because his mother insisted on being present at his interview. Every time the admissions officer would ask a question, the mother would pipe up. The college was worried that the student wouldn't be able to survive his freshman year if they didn't admit his mother as well. (He ended up at another Ivy League college, where he did brilliantly.) What the admissions officer didn't realize was that the student had figured out that the best way to deal with his pushy mom was to let her do what she wanted and not pay any attention. He wasn't dependent on her; she was dependent on him. But that didn't come across. All the admissions officer could see was a mama's boy.

Admissions officers don't like having your mom or dad in the room with you any better than you do. Most will tell parents to wait in the waiting room. But you don't even want this problem to come up. You don't look good if your first contact with an admissions officer involves the admissions officer telling your parents to get lost. If your parents are adamant about wanting to accompany you to your interview itself, don't sign up for an interview.

7. Don't worry about the time.

Students sometimes are told that the sign of a good interview is that it lasts longer than the time allowed for it. Forget about this. During interviewing season, most colleges schedule interviews so tightly that it isn't possible to let one interview run long without screwing up the entire schedule. Don't worry if your interview lasts exactly as long as the secretary said it would. And don't try to stretch out the end of your interview by suddenly becoming long-winded or asking a lot of questions you don't care about.

8. Save the best for last.

If you have interviews at more than one school, you'll get better as you go along. Try to arrange your schedule so that your first interviews are at the schools you care about least or at any rate the schools you are most likely to get into. You can even schedule interviews at schools in which you have no interest at all, just for the practice. Admissions officers frown on this practice for obvious reasons, but they won't find out.

9. Send a thank-you note afterwards.

Always a good idea. Your note can be quite short, but it shouldn't sound mechanical. As with any good thank-you note, mention a specific. And don't suck up. You might ask your mom to read your note before you send it. And remember, no smiley faces.

QUESTIONS AND ANSWERS

Should I include a copy of an A-plus paper from my English class?

No. Many students do this. It almost always backfires. First, admissions officers won't be nearly as interested in your thoughts on *Beowulf* as your English teacher was. Second, if your A-plus paper seems boring and poorly written, an admissions officer will begin to have doubts about all those A's in your transcript. Third, no college admissions officer will be happy to be given *more* to read.

Can I use the same essay on more than one application?

Maybe, although you need to be absolutely certain that the essay fits. Few applications ask exactly the same questions in exactly the same way. Admissions officers are generally familiar with one another's application forms. It will be held against you if you are suspected of trying to double your mileage.

On the other hand, you can probably use at least bits and pieces of the same essay in most or all of your applications. Adapt the material to fit particular questions and particular schools—also particular space requirements. There's no need to start from scratch with every application.

When essay questions are open-ended enough, students sometimes find that they can slip in a composition written for a class. This is usually not a good idea. Class work has a tendency to sound like class work.

I don't care what you say. I'm going to write an essay that's longer than the space allowed for it. What do you think of that, huh?

If you feel you have to do this, write the entire essay on a separate piece of paper and type "See Attached Essay" in the space provided in the application form. This will keep readers from being confused or having to flip back and forth through your folder. At the top of your attached paper, retype the entire essay question from the application. Make sure everything is clear and clearly labeled.

You give a list of bad essay topics. Why don't you give a list of good essay topics?

A good essay topic ceases to be a good essay topic the minute a lot of kids choose it. It becomes a Joe Bloggs essay topic. We do give you a number of suggestions that ought to help you think of interesting topics or approaches, but listing a particular topic in a book effectively kills it. The very best essays are the ones that truly do come from the heart; they don't come from a list. If you follow our guidelines, you should greatly increase your chances of finding a topic or an approach that will show you to your advantage.

If I write a stupid essay, will I ruin my chances?

No. We know of a student who, when asked to write about "a person who has made a difference in your life," filled the entire page with the words "A man called Jesus Christ" in five different colors of crayon. He still got in—and this was a very selective college. That doesn't mean everybody can get away with writing non-essays on forbidden themes in crayon, but it does demonstrate that admissions officers are more understanding of temporary lapses of judgment than they are sometimes believed to be. You shouldn't count on their generosity, though. It's better to be admitted because of your essay than in spite of it.

CHAPTER 6

MINORITIES, RICH KIDS, ARTISTS, ATHLETES, AND OTHER SPECIAL CASES

"I was a pretty big deal on my high school hockey team. I figured I'd go to the state university with a bunch of my buddies. Then, for the hell of it, I applied to Harvard. I didn't have the grades or the scores, but they let me in. They needed a forward."

C ollege admissions decisions are made without regard to race, creed, color, or any other factor that has nothing to do with your qualifications as a student—right? Wrong.

The color of your skin, the size of your family fortune, your religion, your time in the 100-yard dash, and any number of other seemingly extraneous qualities can have a big effect on your chances of being admitted to the school of your choice. Sometimes these factors can help you; sometimes they can harm you. Almost everyone can benefit to some extent by learning what college admissions officers really think.

ETHNIC BACKGROUND

Colleges sometimes claim that their admissions departments are "colorblind" or that they pay no attention to race in deciding who gets in and who is rejected. But this is never true. Ethnic background can make a big difference. Here are some general observations arranged according to particular groups:

BLACKS

Most selective colleges have tiny percentages of black students. There are many reasons for this, including cultural distortions in the SAT and ACT, poor high school preparation, ignorant admissions officers, and the systematic unfairness of the American society. You won't be able to change most of these factors between now and the time you apply to college. But you may be able to change some of them and, in doing so, improve your chances.

Most selective colleges would like to have more black students than they do, if for no other reason than that they very much want to appear to be unprejudiced. Why don't they simply admit more? There are several reasons. The main one is that they worry that black students, who for various reasons generally attend worse high schools than white students do, won't be adequately prepared. One of the main sources of this concern is the SAT, on which blacks as a group score substantially lower than whites. (Blacks as a group score about 100 points lower on each half of the test than whites do.)

Why do blacks do worse than whites on the SAT? No one really knows, but there are clearly a number of reasons. One is a sort of built-in bias in the test. The SAT is a product of white, upper-middle-class culture, and upper-middle-class whites have a distinct advantage on it. In fact, the correlation between the SAT scores and family income is as strong as the correlation between SAT scores and academic performance at many colleges. Another reason is that black high schools tend to have less money, fewer resources, worse teachers, and more problems than white high schools, leaving black students generally less well prepared.

Fortunately, as we said in Chapter Two, the SAT is the one significant part of your record that you can do something about in a short time. Careful preparation for the SAT is important for most students, but it is absolutely essential for black students. Recruiting of black students by selective colleges is based almost entirely on SAT and PSAT scores. Simply scoring above 650 or so on each half of the test would be enough to virtually guarantee you admission at any college in the country.

Here are some other important guidelines:

▪ Make sure the admissions committee knows you're black. (Attach a photograph.) Selective colleges generally have less stringent requirements for black applicants. Take advantage of them.

▪ Don't be afraid to aim high with some of your applications. You may be able to get into schools that wouldn't accept you if you were white.

▪ Investigate the colleges that interest you. Predominantly white colleges can be hostile places for black students, particularly if they are located in predominantly white areas. It is important to find out not only how many black students are admitted but also how many stay on to graduate. If the school has a high attrition rate for blacks (as many do) then you should try to find out what's driving them away.

▪ Talk to black students. Find out what their experience has been. The black population at most selective schools is so small that even talking to a handful of students can give you a fairly complete picture.

ASIAN AMERICANS

There have been a number of newspaper and magazine articles recently about the large numbers of American college students with Japanese, Chinese, Korean, and Vietnamese backgrounds. Many such students have been extraordinarily successful academically, to the point where some colleges now worry that there are "too many" of these students on their campuses. Being an Asian American can now actually be a distinct disadvantage in the admissions processes at some of the most selective schools in the country.

A recent education supplement in the *New York Times* contained an article about the academic success of Asian students in America. Along with the article was a sidebar that underscored the disadvantage faced by Asian Americans. "One consequence of Asian Americans' success, many feel, is that they are forced to compete against one another in disciplines in which they excel," the article said. "At Berkeley, Wang Ling-chi, an associate professor of Asian American Studies, said he knew of several Asian Americans who had been rejected for admission even though their grades were high enough. Each, he said, had wanted to major in electrical engineering, a field already crowded with Asian Americans."

If you are an Asian American—or even if you simply have an Asian or Asian-sounding surname—you need to be careful about what you do and don't say in your application. You need to avoid being an Asian Joe Bloggs.

Asian Joe Bloggs is an Asian American applicant with a very high math SAT score, a low or mediocre verbal SAT score, very high math- or science-related Achievement test scores, high math and science grades, few credits in the humanities, few extracurricular activities, an intended major in math or the sciences, and an ambition to be a doctor, an engineer, or a research scientist. The more you sound like this person, the more likely admissions officers will be to treat you as part of the "Asian invasion" and reject your application.

If you share traits with Asian Joe Bloggs, you should probably pay careful attention to the following guidelines:

- If you're given an option, don't attach a photograph to your application and don't answer the optional question about your ethnic background. This is especially important if you don't have an Asian-sounding surname. (By the same token, if you do have an Asian-sounding surname but aren't Asian, do attach a photograph.)

- Work on your verbal SAT score, take some literature and history courses, and get involved in activities other than math club, chess club, and computer club.

- Do *not* write your application essay about the importance of your family or the positive/negative aspects of living in two cultures. These are Asian Joe Bloggs topics, and they are incredibly popular. Instead, write about something entirely *un*related to your ethnic background.

- Don't say you want to be a doctor and don't say you want to major in math or the sciences. You don't have to lie. If you have lousy SAT verbal scores, saying you want to be an English major isn't going to help you, either. Just say you're undecided. The point is to distance yourself as much as possible from the stereotype.

These guidelines are less important if you are chiefly interested in less selective schools or if you are applying to schools where *all* the students take only math and science courses and dream of medical or research careers. In fact, Asian Joe Bloggs's high math and science scores can be an advantage in applying to schools below the Ivy League level. Even there, though, the less you sound like the stereotype, the better your chances will be.

HISPANICS

Being Hispanic can help you, because admitting you will help a college boost its percentage of minority students. You probably won't be able to pass yourself off as Hispanic, though, if you come from a well-to-do family in Mexico. In general, the guidelines for blacks apply to you: The easiest way to improve your chances is to get your SAT scores up.

If you have a Hispanic surname (because your father is from

Chile, say) but you don't come from a disadvantaged background, don't answer the ethnic-background question on your application.

RELIGION

Columbia University originally adopted admissions testing (early in this century) in an effort to limit the number of Jews in its student body. The directors of the university believed that if admission were based on the results of an intelligence test, fewer Jews would be admitted, because Jews (according to the directors) were clearly less intelligent than non-Jews. As it turned out, the Jews did better on the intelligence test than the non-Jews.

Although this sort of prejudice is less prevalent and less overt than it was in those days, your religious views and religious background can still affect your admissions chances. Generally speaking, unless you are applying to a school with a clear and stated religious orientation, the less you say about your religious views the better. Students with strong religious beliefs— especially strong religious beliefs that they write about in their application essays—tend to make admissions officers nervous. Write about something else.

ARTISTS, MUSICIANS, POETS, ETC.

Colleges often give special treatment to students with special talents. The simple fact that the university orchestra is short an oboe might be enough to get you into Harvard. (Voice and piano are Joe Bloggs instruments, incidentally. If you want to stand out, take harp lessons.)

Many schools allow you to submit paintings, recordings, and so on for special consideration as part of your application. Other schools, such as Stanford, don't. Be sure you know before you send off your portfolio.

Some general guidelines:

- Think small. Send slides, not canvases. Send a *small* selection of your best work, not everything you've ever done. (Comic-book-style drawing doesn't count as art.)

- If your brilliant career as an artist/musician/poet/dancer has brought you into contact with faculty members, consider asking them to recommend you to the admissions committee. One of our students got a powerful recommendation from a poetry professor at a college she wanted to attend. The student had come into contact with the professor in a writing workshop she had attended outside of school. The professor wrote a letter to the admissions committee in support of her, and she was admitted. (She probably would have been admitted anyway, but the letter certainly didn't hurt.) Always follow up with a thank-you note.

- The more professional your slides look, the more impressed the admissions committee will be. This is a corollary of the everything-must-be-typed rule. Have your slides made at a custom photo lab and submit them in the kinds of plastic sleeves professionals use.

- If you submit samples of your creative writing, avoid forbidden themes (sex, drugs, etc.). Submitting creative writing is always risky. Published samples are better than unpublished ones, and outside publications are vastly better than school publications.

- If you submit a tape of your musical performance, be sure it is a standard cassette or meets other specifications stated in the catalogue. While it need not be professionally produced, be sure its quality is as good as possible. (No rock groups.)

- Don't send volumes of reviews, especially if you are a drama student.

- If you are a dancer, see if a videotape would be reviewed by the dance committee. Submit one only if they really welcome it. In your tape, wear traditional dance attire and don't do anything too weird.

ATHLETES

Everyone knows that great athletic ability can win you a big scholarship at a great athletic school. But it can also get you into the Ivy League.

Almost every college in the country gives preferential treatment to accomplished athletes. How accomplished you have to be to be treated preferentially depends on your sport and the school. Your skills as a quarterback might not be enough to win you a scholarship to the University of Alabama, but they might be enough to make Yale overlook your SAT scores. Virtually all schools lower their academic requirements for promising athletes. If you don't have what it takes academically to scrape through Ivy League admissions but do have what it takes athletically to start on an Ivy League football team, you could end up at a better school than you may think. Columbia, for example, has a lousy football team (no victories in eons); a star high school player might very well find his application being read more than once.

You have to be coveted by a coach before you can get this sort of treatment. If you are a serious prospect and the athletic department doesn't know about you already, visit the school and make an appointment with the coach. If a visit is impossible, write a letter. Ask your high school coach or athletic director to help pave the way or at least help you find the names of the people to whom you should write. A strong recommendation from your high school coach is a must.

Pushing too hard on the athletic angle can be dangerous if you aren't college varsity caliber. If you don't look like a serious prospect, an emphasis on sports in your application could make you look like a "dumb jock," even if your grades and scores are pretty good. Being captain of a team will help you anywhere, though, for the reasons we discussed in Chapter Three.

QUESTIONS AND ANSWERS

Isn't it unfair when colleges give minorities special consideration in admissions?

No. What's unfair is an educational system that has consistently denied opportunities to people outside the mainstream of American society. Schools that make an extra effort to extend the privilege of higher education to those formerly denied it are helping to make our society better for everyone.

Is sex a factor in college admissions?

Yes. There aren't many single-sex colleges in the country anymore. Most other colleges aim for equal representation of men and women. This doesn't mean that colleges don't pay attention to the sex of their applicants. Men and women are judged by different criteria, and you can take advantage of this in your applications.

Once again, the Joe Bloggs principle is at the heart of it. A boy whose verbal SAT score is higher than his math SAT score stands out, because he contradicts the stereotype that boys' strengths are mathematical and girls' strengths are verbal. Similarly, the girl who was president of her high school math club looks interesting and unusual, while the boy who was president of his math club may look like a nerd. The same principle applies to entire colleges. MIT, Dartmouth, and Princeton are three schools with strong reputations as male schools. None of these schools enrolls anywhere near as many women as it would like. Because these schools want more women students, women have an advantage in applying. The opposite is true at Vassar. Vassar's image as a school for women persisted after it went coeducational. Men don't apply or enroll at the same rate women do. Thus men have an advantage in admissions—particularly athletes, since male jocks on campus help diminish the school's image as a place for women only.

LEARNING DISABLED

Because LD students get to take the SAT untimed, some students work out the following scam: *If I pretend to be LD, I'll get all this extra time on my SAT!* They figure if they can score 1000 timed, a 1300 without time pressure should be a piece of cake. Wrong.

In the first place, to take an untimed SAT, you have to be diagnosed LD. You can't just decide to take it on a whim. In the second place, taking the SAT untimed does not give everyone a significant advantage. At the Princeton Review, we give any student who is considering an untimed SAT two tests—one timed, the other untimed. By comparing the timed score with the untimed score, we get some idea of whether the student should take the SAT untimed.

If you truly are learning disabled, you have two problems: finding an appropriate school and getting into it. Most colleges aren't set up to deal with serious disabilities. If you have always been given special help, you're going to suffer at a school where no such help is given. Many colleges know this, and avoid LD kids.

Being learning disabled, however, does not prevent you from going to college. Indeed, many colleges welcome LD students. By federal law, a college must accept a learning disabled student if he or she is otherwise qualified.

Not every counselor is intimately acquainted with all the colleges offering LD placement. This is a specialized area, so if your school counselor cannot answer all your questions, seek an outside professional. If you want to get information on your own, visit a college fair given by a school that deals with LD teens. For example, the college fair given by the Hilltop Preparatory School in Rosemont, Pennsylvania, invites only colleges with good LD programs.

All too often college faculty resist working with LD students because they do not understand the learning disabled and their needs. If you have a learning disability, you need a college that is committed to educating people like you. A college whose LD program consists solely of tutoring is *not* doing enough.

When discussing your learning disability with prospective colleges, you must be able to explain your disability precisely. Supply written documentation of a professional diagnosis. You may have to get the college to waive certain course requirements, so you better have hard clinical evidence to support any such request. These documents will help the college provide other services, such as untimed exams or free taped textbooks.

Because you are looking for a good college that will cater to your needs, you should start planning for college earlier than other students. More research is necessary, and campus visits are a must.

CHAPTER 7

FINANCIAL AID

"Student loans look different after graduation than they do before. Now that I've started to have to pay mine off, I wish my financial aid package had been less dependent on loans and more dependent on other sources, like term-time jobs."

In the final analysis, it all boils down to money. Getting into the greatest college in the world won't do you much good if you can't work out a way to pay for it. There are lots of financial aid opportunities out there, but "full rides" are scarce. Putting together a financial package, particularly for one of the most expensive private colleges, takes hard work and sacrifice.

Joe Bloggs has financial difficulties not because financing isn't available but because he doesn't put the necessary time and effort into making it work. You *can* afford a college education, but if money is tight at home you need to take the initiative to find money elsewhere. The sooner you begin researching this subject, the better. Senior year is no time to start thinking about how to pay for a college education.

THINKING ABOUT MONEY

As we told you in Chapter One, money is a crucial consideration. You already knew that, of course, but you should think through the consequences. You may believe that going to Yale is worth any sort of sacrifice, including having to scrub out other students' toilets every morning before class, but maybe you'd be happier *not* scrubbing toilets at the University of Connecticut. No book can answer that sort of question for you. But the time to answer it is now, before you enroll and before you start scrubbing.

DO YOUR HOMEWORK

Unless your family is rolling in money, paying for a private college education takes a lot of hard work: sacrifices from your parents, sacrifices from you, and thorough preparation by all of you before you begin. There's a lot of money out there, but you won't find it unless you look. We strongly suggest that you supplement this book with any of a number of resource books devoted exclusively to securing financial aid. You can find them at your library. The more money you need the more important it is for you to begin researching financial aid as early as possible.

The most useful and complete financial aid guide we've found is:

Lovejoy's Guide to Financial Aid
by Robert Leider
(New York: Monarch Press, 1985, $9.95)

Leider's book is funny and full of solid information. (Leider is dead, but his books are updated by his daughter.)

In addition to reference books outlining sources of financial aid, there are some good books describing relatively low-cost opportunities in education. One of the easiest ways to make it easier to pay for a college education is to get a cheaper college education. Our students have found two books to be especially useful:

The Best Buys in College Education
by Edward B. Fiske
(New York: Times Books, 1985, $9.95)

The Public Ivies
by Richard Moll
(New York: Viking Penguin, Inc., 1985, $9.95)

If you don't believe a good education can be had for less than $15,000 a year, these books will make you think again. There are a number of first-rate colleges and universities in this country that don't have quite the cachet of the Ivy League schools but that offer comparable educations at substantially less cost. If you happen to be lucky enough to live in a state with an excellent university system, you could be in luck.

Fiske offers many examples of good schools with price tags that won't stop your heart. For example, did you know that Cornell University—an Ivy League school—consists of four private colleges and three public colleges in the State University of New York system? As Fiske writes, "For $5,000 less than the cost of the privately endowed segments of Cornell the SUNY student gets some bang for the buck: access to superb facilities, faculty, and libraries on one of the most beautiful campuses in America; an aggressive and overachieving group of friends;

and a salable Ivy League degree that makes it a bargain unique among American universities. 'I receive a specialized education in a small institution and still benefit from the social, cultural, and academic advantages of a major university,' says one woman."

THE OPPOSITE IS ALSO TRUE

You should remember, though, that the nation's richest, most elite private universities aren't just for the rich and elite. Students from families with modest incomes often assume that the Ivy League is out of their league financially. In fact, it is the wealthy schools that have the most money to spend on financial aid. If you have the necessary academic credentials, you may be pleasantly surprised to find that the most prestigious school on your list is also the one that offers you the most attractive aid package. It doesn't always happen that way, of course, but it is *always* true that private schools with small endowments have a much harder time providing aid to those who need it. Rich schools can be more generous than poor ones.

STAY UP TO DATE

The financial aid picture is changing all the time. Changes in tuition, changes in aid opportunities, and changes in tax laws can make good books obsolete in a hurry. Always check the copyright date of any financial aid reference book you find in the library. A book or edition that's even a year or two old can be misleading. Look for current books or updated editions.

Also pay close attention to the financial aid information provided by the colleges to which you are interested in applying. Colleges interested in attracting applications (in other words, all colleges) are constantly coming up with innovative approaches to financing. Bard College, in Annandale-on-Hudson, New York, has a new program that permits a few students each year to attend Bard, an expensive private school, for what it would have cost them to attend their own state universities. This has been Bard's response to the increasing attractiveness of the generally less expensive state schools. As the competition for students increases in coming years, you can expect to see many such innovative offers. Expensive colleges know they have to make it easier for their students to pay if they want to keep filling their dormitories. Many of these new approaches and innovations may be too new to be described in even the most up-to-date college guide. You'll have to look for information from the colleges themselves.

MONEY, MONEY, MONEY

As we have said before, no college is truly "needblind" in weighing applications. Your ability to pay can affect or even determine your chance of being admitted. Some colleges sift through their tentative acceptances before mailing them and weed out marginal candidates with big aid needs. A bigger contribution from your family may improve your chances of being admitted.

You should keep this in mind as you and your family sit down to determine how much you will be able to pay. Most financial aid guides emphasize methods for *decreasing* your outright contribution and *increasing* your eligibility for loans and other forms of aid. Obviously, doing so can lessen the immediate financial strain on your family. But it can also harm your admissions chances. If it comes down to a choice between you and a student who can pay his own way, the advantage will belong to the student who can pay.

The point is not that your family should put itself in financial jeopardy in order to pay more up front for your education, but that you should be honest and realistic as you assess your needs. Many strategies for approaching financial aid involve hiding family assets so that a student will look poorer than he or she is and qualify for a more generous aid package. In doing this you need to be careful about weighing the advantages and disadvantages. Qualifying for more aid won't help if your apparent aid requirements make you impossible for a school to admit.

You should also remember that the more you pay up front,

the less your financial burden will be in coming years. Student loans have to be paid back. As many as half of the students who graduate from college this year will graduate in debt. The federal government's Guaranteed Student Loan program lent more than $50 billion in 1986—money that will eventually have to be paid back with interest. Recent college graduates often have the feeling that they go to work only to pay taxes and pay off their college debts. Once those two items are taken care of, there often isn't much left for the other things in life—such as food and rent.

PRE-MEDS BEWARE!

Keeping your debt burden to a minimum is especially important if you plan to go on to graduate or professional school. Suppose you want to be a dentist. After four years of college you have four or five years of dental school. By the time you're ready to begin practicing, you could easily be a hundred thousand dollars in debt. If you want to go into private practice, you could easily go *another* hundred thousand dollars in the red just setting up your office. Then, of course, you'll need a place to live. . . .

HOW IT WORKS

Applying to college with a need for financial aid is a two-step process: You apply for admission and you apply for aid. If a college does admit you and offer you aid, that aid will usually be geared to your need. What generally happens is that the college takes its own cost, subtracts the amount you and your family are able to contribute, subtracts the amount of other awards and scholarships you may be entitled to, and either does or doesn't make up the rest. The amount provided by the college can come in many forms. Depending on the college's resources and policies as well as on your need, all or part of the college's commitment might be an outright grant, a loan, or a guaranteed job for you on campus during the school year.

THE COLLEGE BOARD AND ETS AGAIN

How do colleges know how much your family can afford to contribute? You remember the College Board and ETS—the companies that bring you the SAT. What you may not realize is that they also bring you the Financial Aid Form (FAF), a "needs analysis" questionnaire used by many colleges to determine eligibility for financial aid. Other colleges use the Family Financial Statement (FFS), which is published and evaluated by the American College Testing Program, the company that brings you the ACT. These forms are generally required *in addition to* the college's own financial aid form, which is usually part of its application. Your guidance counselor should have copies of both the FAF and FFS. Get cracking.

BE EARLY

As always, beware of creeping deadlines. Your various financial aid forms may not all be due at the same time, and they may be due at different times from your general application. Even more important, your chances of receiving an attractive aid offer, or any offer at all, may depend on how early you submit your forms. Colleges have a tendency to be more generous with aid early in the process and gradually to become stingy as resources are depleted. If you wait till the last minute, the college may have nothing left to offer you. This can also affect your chances of admission. Faced with the choice of rejecting you or accepting you with an inadequate aid offer, the college may elect to reject you.

WHAT ARE ALL THESE FORMS LIKE?

FAF and FFS ask for a lot of confidential information. You and your parents will have to answer questions about your family's income, savings, taxes, expenses, and other personal matters. You'll have to provide such information as the age of your parents, the number of siblings living at home, medical expenses not paid by insurance, welfare benefits, the purchase price of your home, and the amount of state and local taxes paid. Families often feel as though they've been interrogated by the FBI by the time they come to the end. Your parents may feel that they've had to reveal just about everything about themselves that there is to reveal.

All this personal information is analyzed by people at ETS or ACTP, and an analysis of it, along with an estimate of your family's ability to pay, is sent to colleges and others you specify (for a fee, of course) in much the same way that your SAT or ACT scores are reported. You will also receive a summary of your report. Be sure to check it for errors, which are not uncommon.

FAF and FFS also have boxes that you can check if you want to be considered for various federal and state aid programs. You should do so—but don't forget that many such programs have other requirements as well. Do your homework. FFS has recently been made more comprehensive, enabling you to do the equivalent of "one-stop shopping" for financial aid. FAF will probably follow suit. This makes sense. Virtually all financial aid programs want to know the same information about you. It doesn't make sense to have to fill out essentially the same form over and over again. The process could easily be streamlined, and undoubtedly it will be. As the case of FFS shows, this has already begun to happen.

SOURCES OF AID

There are many sources of financial aid. Some you know about already, some you probably don't. As we mentioned earlier, a financial aid package usually breaks down into three parts: outright grants (from the college itself or from outside sources), loans, and guaranteed jobs on campus. The constant in every package is your family's contribution. If you suddenly win a thousand-dollar scholarship from the local Lions' Club, the thousand dollars won't go to your parents, enabling them to reduce their contribution; it will go to the college. Obviously, the more money you can get in the form of an outright grant of some kind, the better off you're going to be, because that money won't have to be paid back later on.

ALL OFFERS ARE NOT EQUAL

The composition of an aid package is at least as important as the total amount. Suppose your family can afford to contribute $4,000 a year to your college education, and you've been accepted by two schools whose costs are approximately $8,000 a year. Both schools come up with aid packages worth $4,000 a year. But the packages are not the same. Here's how they break down:

Package A	*Package B*
Outright grant: $2,000	Outright grant: $3,000
Campus job: $1,000	Campus job: $1,000
Loan: $1,000	

College A expects you to borrow $1,000. This loan is part of the financial aid equation for that school. College B, however, wants you badly enough to offer you $3,000 outright. In combination with a job worth $1,000, this takes care of your financial needs—and you'll graduate without debt.

Weighing financial aid offers can get a lot more complicated than that. You and your parents will have to work together closely and think realistically about the consequences of your decisions. The more attractive you are to a school in comparison with other applicants, the sweeter their aid offer is likely to be. Deciding which offer to accept is often a matter of deciding between a better school and a better aid package. (Financial aid packages are sometimes negotiable. Ask you guidance counselor to inquire.)

SOURCES OF AID II

The following is a survey of the most important sources of financial aid. We'll cover the more unusual sources first, and

131

then get down to the nitty-gritty of things like government entitlement programs and sources of loans.

UNUSUAL SOURCES

SCHOLARSHIPS THROUGH TESTING, PART ONE

If you take Advanced Placement courses and do well on the tests, you could earn—regardless of your financial need—the equivalent of an outright grant worth twenty-five percent of your four-year college costs, including tuition, room and board, books, beer, expenses, and everything else.

How?

Simply by doing well enough on your AP tests to earn academic credits at the college where you enroll. Students with top AP scores are sometimes awarded as much as a full year's worth of college credit. This enables them to graduate in three years and save a full year's worth of college costs.

Not all colleges do this, but many do. And some grant credit for AP scores that are really quite low. Granting AP credit lets the colleges feel generous: They can give the equivalent of big scholarships at no cost to themselves. And for students, the potential return on an investment in AP test fees is enormous. The only negative consideration is that starting college as a sophomore can be disorienting (also less fun—three years of fooling around instead of four). But the AP program remains a source of financial aid that many students overlook.

AP tests, naturally, are a College Board/ETS program. A similar program, run by the same people, is the College Level Examination Program (CLEP). CLEP tests are extremely easy, and the colleges that accept them for credit tend not to be very rigorous, but if you're applying to one of those colleges, keep the tests in mind. Almost anybody should be able to rack up a semester or two of "college credit" by taking CLEP exams.

SCHOLARSHIPS THROUGH TESTING, PART TWO

The PSAT, which is usually given early in junior year, not only gives you practice for the SAT but also enters you in an aid lottery called the National Merit Scholarship Program. Students who score extremely well on the test may qualify for scholarships of various kinds, some of which are based on need and some of which are not. Even if you don't win money, being designated a finalist, semifinalist, or letter of commendation winner can improve your admission chances substantially. Get the details from your guidance counselor (and practice for the PSAT).

Some colleges now offer outright awards to students who score high on the PSAT or SAT, regardless of their financial need. Others offer scholarships based on high class ranks. These awards are essentially a marketing tool: The schools that offer them are typically competitive, sub-Ivy League schools that want to make themselves look more selective by enrolling some students with big test scores. If you have a knack for taking ETS tests, it can be worth a good deal of money. Talk to your guidance counselor, check the library, and read the information colleges send you.

THE MILITARY

"We're not a company; we're your country." Ever since the creation of the GI Bill, which enabled returning soldiers to attend college at the end of World War II, military service has provided a way for young people to pay for college educations. Of course, there's a very big string attached: You have to pay for your financial aid by serving in the military. A military commitment is no joke. It lasts a long time, once you've signed up for it you can't weasel your way out of it, and, depending on the state of the world, you could get shot at. But there are rewards as well. For example, enlisting in the Army Reserve could entitle you to as much as $16,000 towards a college education. You might even discover that you enjoy being a soldier (you can retire after twenty years at half pay). Check with a local recruiter.

THE COLLEGES THEMSELVES

As colleges have become more and more competitive in their search for good students (or for any students at all), they have also become more innovative and aggressive in devising ways to help students pay their tuitions. Some of the current offerings: flexible payment plans, inexpensive loans, prepayment plans, extended payment plans. The University of Detroit, for example, offers discounted tuitions to parents willing to pay in advance. Parents with a newborn infant this year could buy their child four years at Detroit eighteen years from now for less than $5,000. The older the child, the higher the cost—though the bottom line is always smaller than the projected tuition. That may sound like a good deal to some (hundreds have already signed up), but there are many drawbacks. One of the biggest is that you have to go to the University of Detroit. If Junior decides in 2005 that he'd really rather go to Dartmouth, his parents will get their original stake back but not the accumulated interest.

Sorting through these innovative plans requires a good bit of homework. Many are just gimmicks designed to attract attention. But some are genuinely helpful to parents in need. It's worth remembering that colleges need students just as much as students need degrees. Read the brochures and ask questions if you are confused.

SOURCES OF LOANS

There is roughly $17 billion available each year in loans either subsidized or guaranteed by the federal government. More loans are available from state governments, still more are available from banks and other financial institutions, and even more are available from colleges. Now, if only you didn't have to pay them back. . . .

GUARANTEED STUDENT LOANS (GSL)

These are relatively low-interest loans guaranteed and subsidized by the federal government. The rate is currently 8 percent. If you are eligible, you can borrow up to $2,500 a year (no more than $12,500 altogether), pay no interest while you're in school or for six months after you graduate (taxpayers pick up the tab), and take ten years to pay the money back. GSLs are also available for graduate students.

There are a number of restrictions and requirements. Generally speaking, families with incomes under $30,000 qualify automatically for the full amount; families with incomes over $30,000 have to demonstrate need and meet certain other tests. The higher a family's income, the less likely that it will be able to borrow the maximum amount. All GSLs are subject to a 5-percent "origination fee," which is what bankers charge you for giving you the privilege of paying them to lend you money. The origination fee makes the true cost of the loan higher than the quoted 8-percent rate. It also has to be paid up front (it will be deducted from the loan amount), although in actual dollars the amount isn't incredibly onerous: 5 percent of $2,500 is $125.

One way to pay back GSLs: Enlist. Service in the National Guard, Reserves, or any branch of the regular military can earn you partial or full payment of your debt. Spend three years in the army and you could retire your full GSL debt.

GSL applications are available from banks, the government, and college financial aid officers. Your high school guidance counselor can probably help as well. The program (along with four others) is explained in a free booklet called *The Student Guide: Five Federal Financial Aid Programs*. It's published by the government. You can request a copy from The Department of Education, 400 Maryland Ave., SWE, Room 1059, Washington, DC 20202. Do that right now.

For a list of lenders in your state, contact the appropriate agency below:

Alabama
Commission on Higher Education
One Court Square, Suite 221
Montgomery, AL 36197

Alaska
Alaska Commission on Postsecondary Education
Pouch FP, 400 Willoughby Ave.
Juneau, AK 99811

Arizona
Arizona Educational Loan Program
Phelps Dodge Tower, Suite 621
2600 N. Central Ave.
Phoenix, AZ 85004

Arkansas
Student Loan Guarantee Foundation of Arkansas
1515 W. Seventh St., Suite 515
Little Rock, AR 72202

California
California Student Aid Commission
1410 Fifth St.
Sacramento, CA 95814

Colorado
Colorado Guaranteed Student Loan Program
7000 Broadway, Suite 100
Denver, CO 90221

Connecticut
Connecticut Student Loan Foundation
25 Pratt St.
Hartford, CT 06103

Delaware
Delaware Higher Education Loan Program
c/o Brandywine College
P.O. Box 7139
Wilmington, DE 19803

District of Columbia
Higher Education Assistance Foundation
1030 Fifteenth St., NW, Suite 1000
Washington, DC 20005

Florida
Florida Student Financial Assistance Commission
Knott Building
Tallahassee, FL 32301

Georgia
Georgia Higher Education Assistance Corporation
2082 E. Exchange Pl., Suite 200
Tucker, GA 30084

Hawaii
Hawaii Educational Loan Program
1314 S. King St.
Honolulu, HI 96814

Idaho
SLFI Processing Center
P.O. Box 730
Fruitland, ID 83619

Illinois
Illinois Guaranteed Loan Program
102 Wilmot Rd.
Deerfield, IL 60015

Indiana
State Student Assistance Commission of Indiana
219 N. Senate Ave.
Indianapolis, IN 46202

Iowa
Iowa College Aid Commission
201 Jewett Bldg.
9th Street and Grande Avenue
Des Moines, IA 50309

Kansas
Higher Education Assistance Foundation
34 Corporate Woods, Suite 270
10950 Grandview Dr.
Overland Park, KS 66210

Kentucky
Kentucky Higher Education Assistance Authority
1050 U.S. 127 South
West Frankfort Office Complex
Frankfort, KY 40601

Louisiana
Governor's Special Commission on Educational Services
P.O. Box 44127, Capitol Station
Baton Rouge, LA 70804

Maine
State Department of Educational and Cultural Services
Education Building
Augusta, ME 04333

Maryland
Maryland Higher Education Loan Corporation
2100 Guilford Ave.
Baltimore, MD 21218

Massachusetts
Massachusetts Higher Education Assistance Authority
330 Stuart St.
Boston, MA 02116

Michigan
Michigan Higher Education Assistance Authority
P.O. Box 30047
Lansing, MI 48909

Minnesota
Higher Education Assistance Foundation
1600 American National Bank Building
Fifth and Minnesota Streets
St. Paul, MN 55101

Mississippi
Mississippi Guaranteed Student Loan Agency
Institutions of Higher Learning
3825 Ridgewood, P. O. Box 342
Jackson, MS 38205

Missouri
Missouri Coordinating Board for Higher Education
P.O. Box 1438
Jefferson City, MO 65102

Montana
Commission on Higher Education
33 S. Last Chance Gulch
Helena, MT 59620

Nebraska
Higher Education Assistance Foundation
Cornhusker Bank, #304
11th and Cornhusker Highway
Lincoln, NE 68521

Nevada
Nevada Higher Education Student Loan Program
Department of Education
400 W. King St.
Carson City, NV 89710

New Hampshire
New Hampshire Higher Education Assistance Foundation
143 N. Main St.
P.O. Box 877
Concord, NH 03301

New Jersey
New Jersey Higher Education Assistance Authority
CN 00543
Trenton, NJ 08625

New Mexico
New Mexico Educational Assistance Foundation
2301 Yale, SE, Building C
Albuquerque, NM 87106

New York
New York State Higher Education Services Corporation
99 Washington Ave.
Albany, NY 12255

North Carolina
North Carolina State Education Assistance Authority
P.O. Box 2688
Chapel Hill, NC 27514

North Dakota
Bank of North Dakota
700 Main St., Drawer 1657
Bismarck, ND 58501

Ohio
Ohio Student Loan Commission
P.O. Box 16610
Columbus, OH 43216

Oklahoma
Oklahoma State Regents for Higher Education
500 Education Building
State Capitol Complex
Oklahoma City, OK 73105

Oregon
Oregon State Scholarship Commission
1445 Willamette St.
Eugene, OR 97401

Pennsylvania
Pennsylvania Higher Education Assistance Agency
600 Boas St., Towne House
Harrisburg, PA 17102

Rhode Island
Rhode Island Higher Education Assistance Authority
274 Weybosset St., Room 402
Providence, RI 02903

South Carolina
South Carolina Student Loan Corporation
Interstate Center, Suite 210
P.O. Box 21487
Columbia, SC 29221

South Dakota
Education Assistance Corporation
115 First Ave., SW
Aberdeen, SD 57401

Tennessee
Tennessee Student Assistance Corporation
B-3 Capitol Towers, Suite 9
Nashville, TN 37219

Texas
Texas Guaranteed Student Loan Corporation
P.O. Box 15996
Austin, TX 78761

Utah
Education Loan Services, Inc.
P.O. Box 31802
Salt Lake City, UT 84131

Vermont
Student Assistance Corporation
P.O. Box 2000
Winooski, VT 05404

Virginia
State Education Assistance Authority
6 N. Sixth St., Suite 300
Richmond, VA 23219

Washington
Student Loan Guaranty Association
500 Colman Building
811 First Ave.
Seattle, WA 98104

West Virginia
Higher Education Assistance Foundation
P.O. Box 591
Charleston, WV 25322

Wisconsin
Higher Education Corporation
137 E. Wilson St.
Madison, WI 53702

Wyoming
Higher Education Assistance Foundation
American National Bank Building, Suite 320
20th Street at Capitol
Cheyenne, WY 82001

Guam
United Student Aid Funds, Inc.
1314 S. King St.
Honolulu, HI 96814

Puerto Rico
Puerto Rico Higher Education Assistance Corporation
P.O. Box 42001
Minillas Station
San Juan, PR 00940

Virgin Islands
Board of Education
P.O. Box 9128
St. Thomas, VI 00801

PARENT LOANS FOR UNDERGRADUATE STUDENTS (PLUS)

These are loans available to anyone, no matter what their income. The interest rate is higher (currently 12 percent, about the same as an ordinary consumer loan). The maximum loan is $3,000 per year for a total of no more than $15,000. Repayment period is ten years, but there is no interest subsidy and repayment begins immediately. Similar loans are available under the same program for independent students (those not supported by parents) and graduate students.

PLUS loans are not the greatest deals in the world. Bankers aren't wild about them and you can be turned down for any of a number of reasons.

NATIONAL DIRECT STUDENT LOANS (NDSL)

These are loans made by colleges with money provided by the federal government. The interest rate is quite low—currently 5 percent. Students can borrow up to $3,000 in their first two years in college, and as much as $6,000 during an entire undergraduate program. Additional funds are available for graduate students. As with GSLs, interest payments are picked up by the government during school and repayment doesn't begin until after graduation. Colleges have some flexibility in deciding which of their students qualify for these loans; generally speaking, your family must earn less than $30,000 and meet several other criteria.

These are great loans if you qualify—the interest rate is hard to beat.

STATE LOANS

All states make loans and other aid to college students. Most such aid is dependent on your attending a school within the state, or some similar restriction. Some states provide aid and other incentives to, for example, medical students who agree to remain within the state following graduation. Other states offer scholarships to good students who attend school within the state. Check with your guidance counselor, a financial aid officer, or with the appropriate state agency. The state agencies are the same ones listed above in the section on Guaranteed Student Loans, with the following exceptions:

Arizona
Commission for Postsecondary Education
1937 W. Jefferson St.
Phoenix, AZ 85009

Arkansas
Department of Higher Education
1301 W. Seventh St.
Little Rock, AR 72201

Colorado
Colorado Commission on Higher Education
1300 Broadway, Second Floor
Denver, CO 80203

Connecticut
Student Financial Assistance Commission
Board of Higher Education
61 Woodland Street
Hartford, CT 06105

Delaware
Delaware Postsecondary Education Commission
State Office Building
820 French St.
Wilmington, DE 19801

District of Columbia
Office of State Education Affairs
1331 H St., NW, Room 600
Washington, DC 20005

Hawaii
Hawaii State Postsecondary Education Commission
Bachman Hall, Room 124
2444 Dole St.
Honolulu, HI 96822

Idaho
State Board of Education
650 W. State St.
Boise, ID 83720

Illinois
State Scholarship Commission
102 Wilmot Road
Deerfield, IL 60015

Kansas
Board of Regents
100 Merchants National Bank Tower
Topeka, KS 66612

Maryland
State Scholarship Board
2100 Guilford Ave.
Baltimore, MD 21218

Massachusetts
Board of Regents of Higher Education
Scholarship Office
330 Stuart Street
Boston, MA 02116

Michigan
Michigan Higher Education Assistance Authority
P.O. Box 30008
Lansing, MI 48909

Minnesota
Minnesota Higher Education Coordinating Board
Capitol Square Building, Suite 400
550 Cedar St.
St. Paul, MN 55101

Mississippi
Post-Secondary Education
Financial Assistance Board
P.O. Box 2336
Jackson, MS 39225

Nebraska
Nebraska Coordinating Commission for Postsecondary
    Education
301 Centennial Mall South
P.O. Box 95005
Lincoln, NE 68509

Nevada
Financial Aid Office
University of Nevada, Reno
Room 200 TSSC
Reno, NV 89557

New Hampshire
New Hampshire Postsecondary Education Commission
61 S. Spring St.
Concord, NH 03301

New Jersey
Department of Higher Education
Office of Student Assistance
4 Quakerbridge Plaza, CN 540
Trenton, NJ 08625

New Mexico
Board of Educational Finance
1068 Cerrillos Rd.
Santa Fe, NM 87503

North Dakota
Student Financial Assistance Program
Capitol Building, 10th Floor
Bismarck, ND 58505

Ohio
Ohio Board of Regents
30 E. Broad St., 36th Floor
Columbus, OH 43215

South Carolina
South Carolina Tuition Grants Agency
P.O Box 11638
Columbia, SC 29211

South Dakota
Department of Education and Cultural Affairs
Kneip Building
Pierre, SD 57501

Texas
Coordinating Board, Texas College and University System
P.O. Box 12788, Capitol Station
Austin, TX 78711

Utah
Utah State Board of Regents
Suite 204
807 E. South Temple
Salt Lake City, UT 84102

Virginia
Council of Higher Education
James Monroe Building
101 N. Fourteenth St.
Richmond, VA 23219

West Virginia
Higher Educational Aids Board
P.O. Box 4007
Charleston, WV 24304

Wisconsin
Higher Educational Aids Board
137 E. Wilson St.
Madison, WI 53702

Wyoming
University of Wyoming
Student Financial Aids
Box 3335, University Station
Laramie, WY 82071

Guam
Student Financial Assistance
University of Guam
P.O. Box EK
Agana, Guam 98910

Puerto Rico
Council on Higher Education
Box F, University of Puerto Rico Station
Rio Piedras, PR 00931

Virgin Islands
Board of Education
O.V. No. 11
St. Thomas, VI 00801

COMMERCIAL LOANS
Banks are in the business of lending money, of course. If you
have to go the ordinary bank route, though, you generally leave

the world of below-market interest rates. Many banks do have programs aimed directly at the college-bound, however. Two examples are the Knight Insurance Agency Extended Repayment Plan (current rate: 10.25 percent) and the Mellon Bank Edu-Check Program (current rate: 12.4 percent). Check with your bank.

SOURCES OF OUTRIGHT GRANTS

PELL GRANTS

Pell grants are cash grants from the federal government paid to undergraduate students from low-income families who meet certain requirements. The formula used by the government to determine eligibility for Pell grants is too complicated to describe. Fortunately, though, you can apply for one simply by checking the appropriate box on your FAF or FFS. You should do this even if you are certain you don't qualify; colleges generally require financial aid candidates to apply for Pell grants, no matter what. If you do qualify, your Pell grant will become the foundation on which your aid package is built.

CLUBS AND ORGANIZATIONS

Lions Clubs, alumni groups, garden clubs, many civic and other organizations provide scholarship money for college students. Such awards are usually small. You shouldn't waste a lot of time scouring the countryside for a few hundred dollars. But be aware of opportunities in your own backyard. If the Loyal Brotherhood of Hyenas has a scholarship, and your father is a Loyal Hyena, you could be in luck.

You should also be aware that many companies—including, perhaps, the ones your mom and dad work for—provide money for college. Your own employer may even have such a program. Check around.

QUESTIONS AND ANSWERS

Should I hire a scholarship search service?

No. These services are expensive and they usually don't provide you with anything you couldn't have found all by yourself in an hour or two at the library. No one is going to drop a big juicy scholarship in your lap. The only dependable way to secure financial aid is to do the homework yourself (although families sometimes find that good accountants can be extremely helpful).

Is a college education really worth all the trouble it takes to get one?

Well, now we're really straying beyond the range of this book. We all went to college, and we all thought it was worth it.

T̲H̲E̲ P̲RINCETON R̲EVIEW

IF YOU'D LIKE MORE INFORMATION

Princeton Review sites are in dozens of cities around the country. For the office nearest you, see the following list.

PRINCETON REVIEW

Arizona
All locations   602/952-8850

California
Orange County (Anaheim area)
     714/553-9411
Los Angeles area   213/474-0909
San Diego area   619/454-2255
San Jose area (Silicon Valley)
     408/268-9674
San Francisco & Marin County
     415/891-9077

Colorado
All locations   303/428-8000

Connecticut
Fairfield County   203/775-4642
Hartford area   203/651-3557
New Haven area   203/775-4642

District of Columbia
All locations   202/797-1410

Florida
All locations   305/445-3933

Georgia
All locations   404/233-0980

Illinois
Chicago area   312/472-1313

Maine
All locations   603/433-7090

Maryland
All locations   202/797-1410

Massachusetts
Amherst area   413/584-6849
Boston area   617/277-5280
Worcester   617/277-5280

Michigan
All locations   313/851-1133

Minnesota
All locations   612/870-1962

Missouri
St. Louis area   314/968-9455

New Hampshire
All locations   603/433-7090

New Jersey

Camden area	215/923-2077
All other locations	609/683-0082

New York

New York City	212/874-7600
	718/935-0091
Long Island	516/935-2999
Westchester & Rockland	
	914/997-1311

Upstate

Albany area	518/458-8552
Binghamton area	607/773-0311
Ithaca area	607/272-4687
Putnam & Duchess	914/997-1311
Syracuse area	315/476-8378

North Carolina

All locations	919/967-7209

Ohio

All locations	617/794-1035

Pennsylvania

Philadelphia area	215/923-2077
Pittsburgh area	413/362-1052

Rhode Island

All locations	401/861-5080

Texas

Austin area	512/469-6336
Dallas area	214/890-0099
Fort Worth area	817/335-4111
Houston area	713/688-5500
San Antonio area	512/341-1942

Vermont

All locations	802/658-6653

Virginia

All locations	202/797-1410

Washington (State)

All locations	206/325-1341

ALL OTHER LOCATIONS

800/333-0369

About the Authors

ADAM ROBINSON was born in 1955. He graduated from Wharton before earning a law degree at Oxford University in England. Robinson, a rated chess master, devised and perfected the now-famous "Joe Bloggs" approach to beating standardized tests in 1980, as well as numerous other core Princeton Review techniques. A free-lance author of many books, Robinson has collaborated with The Princeton Review to develop a number of its courses.

JOHN KATZMAN was born in 1959. He graduated from Princeton University in 1980. After working briefly on Wall Street, he founded The Princeton Review in 1981. Beginning with nineteen high school students in his parents' apartment, Katzman now oversees courses that prepare tens of thousands of high school and college students annually for tests including the SAT, GRE, GMAT, and LSAT.

Both authors live in New York City.